The *New Science Library* presents traditional topics from a modern perspective, particularly those associated with the hard sciences—physics, biology, and medicine—and those of the human sciences—psychology, sociology, and philosophy. The aim of this series is the enrichment of both the scientific and spiritual view of the world through their mutual dialogue and exchange. New Science Library is an imprint of Shambhala Publications.

General Editor: Ken Wilber
Consulting Editors: Jeremy Hayward
                       Francisco Varela

One of the most important books of our time . . . sophisticated, readable, practical. I cannot recommend it too highly. *The Open Mind*

Staying Alive is a lesson in optimism, denying the prevalent pessimistic attitude that suffering and holocaust are inevitable. It is a noble effort . . . Take this opportunity. Begin *Staying Alive*. *The Minnesota Daily*

This superb short book deserves to be singled out for special attention . . . exceptionally readable, deserves the serious attention of everyone seeking to assure the survival of humanity. Jerome Frank, M.D.

Walsh's keen mind, sincerity, and sense of urgency, coupled with the fact that the royalties are used to support human survival programs, makes this book a must. *Common Boundary*

Dr. Walsh offers us a refreshing and hopeful approach to the problems of our times. *Momentum* (National Catholic Educators Association)

. . . a brief but stunning work. *Mind-Expander*

The beginning of a psychology of human survival that Walsh sketches is exciting. It's peppered with good sense and wisdom. It's balanced and sensible, positive and clever. . . . If you read one book in the next twelve months, I hope it's this one. *Fellowship*

Walsh writes with eloquence and conviction. *The Futurist*

. . . a book on global psychology that every political activist should have at his or her fingertips. *New Options*

. . . a wise and hopeful volume. . . . The author helps us take the first and most important step toward ensuring the continuation of our species and life itself. National Association for the Improvement of Community College Teaching *Newsletter*

No book can have greater relevance today than that of Roger Walsh. . . . It is a book that should be read by as many people as possible for its impact would be tremendous and do much to improve the world.
School Psychology International

. . . in this current sea of "nuclear arms" literature, *Staying Alive* may be the one to read. *San Francisco Chronicle*

Staying Alive

THE PSYCHOLOGY OF HUMAN SURVIVAL

ROGER WALSH, M.D.

NEW SCIENCE LIBRARY
Shambhala • Boston & London • 1984

NEW SCIENCE LIBRARY
An imprint of Shambhala Publications, Inc.
314 Dartmouth Street
Boston, Massachusetts 02116

Distributed in the United States by Random House and in Canada by Random House of Canada Ltd.

Printed in the United States of America

Library of Congress Cataloging in Publication Data
Walsh, Roger N.
  Staying alive.
  (New science library)
  1. Disasters—Psychological aspects. 2. Survival (After airplane accidents, ship-wrecks, etc.)—Psychological aspects. 3. Stress (Psychology) 4. Threat (Psychology) 5. Social psychology. I. Title. II. Series.
  BF789.D5W32 1984   155.9   84-5482
  ISBN 0-87773-293-0 (pbk.)
  ISBN 0-394-72690-1 (Random House : pbk.)

TABLE OF CONTENTS

PART 4: LIVING ON THE BRINK

This book is dedicated

To all those who hunger, and are without food.

To all those who thirst, and are without water.

To all those who lie sick, and are without medicine.

To all those who go cold, and are without clothing or shelter.

To all who yearn to understand, and are without education.

To all who are oppressed, and yearn for freedom.

To all those who, out of ignorance and fear, cause suffering.

To all those who suffer, and are without help.

And to all of you, who would help.

FOREWORD

by His Holiness the Dalai Lama

I feel that the present crisis that faces the world is a very real one, and one which concerns the whole of humanity. The survival of civilisation itself is in the balance. Consequently, there is no way to overemphasize the importance of working towards greater harmony and understanding amongst different peoples, and of awakening a wider awareness in the world of the urgent need for peace.

I therefore welcome this book *Staying Alive*, as I always appreciate very deeply any effort made towards creating a more peaceful world. The contribution of the individual to global peace is a crucial one. It is only by generating a greater concern for peace in the minds of more and more people, through endeavors like this book, that the change in attitude so necessary for peace will take place.

Tenzin Gyatso,
the xivth Dalai Lama
Dharamsala

FOREWORD

by Linus Pauling

Roger Walsh, in his book *Staying Alive: The Psychology of Human Survival*, has made a valuable contribution to the effort to improve the world. Every thoughtful reader of the book will find that his life is changed by it to some extent.

We are now at a period in the history of the human race when the world is faced with great problems. Roger Walsh points out that for the first time the problems that we are faced with are those that we ourselves have made. The problems include those presented by the population explosion, mass malnutrition, and other global threats to human survival and well being, and also, as the greatest of all, the possibility that civilization will be destroyed in a nuclear war. There is a good chance that the global threats could be handled if the great nations, together with the smaller nations, were to collaborate in the attacks on them. So long as the present policy of confrontation between the United States and the Soviet Union continues, and so long as a great fraction of the world's wealth is wasted on militarism, there is no possibility of solving the problems.

Roger Walsh points out that our thinking may determine the fate of the world. One aspect of our thinking is that many of us do not recognize that the people in the Soviet Union, with far greater experience with war than the people in the United States, are far more fearful of war. Moreover, with a gross national product only half of the United States and a military budget nearly equal to that of the United States, the burden of militarism is much greater for the Soviet Union than for the United States. It is the recognition of the fact that the cold war puts greater pressure on the Soviet Union than on the United States that is responsible for the continuing increase in our military budget, which, it is planned will involve a total expenditure of 1.9 trillion dollars during the next five years.

Another aspect of our thinking is that we have been misled by our government, which has relied on a sequence of false alarms (the "missile gap," the "window of vulnerability") to direct the thinking of the American people into support of the policy of confrontation.

This book can help us to see for ourselves that our own future and the future of the human race depend upon our willingness and ability to cooperate, to work together in a worldwide attack on the great world problems.

Linus Pauling
Palo Alto, California

ACKNOWLEDGMENTS

The author would like to thank the many people who provided encouragement, stimulation, and feedback. Those include especially William Andrew, Bill Bridges, Elizabeth Campbell, Leslie Clark, Arthur Deikman, Duane Elgin, Dan Ellsberg, Pat Ellsberg, Gordon Globus, Edgar Heim, Gary Lapid, John Levy, Rollo May, Fred McGuire, Don Michaels, Alan Nelson, John O'Neil, Ruth Reynolds, Ken Ring, Tom Roberts, Vic Gioschia, Guy de Mallac, and particularly Frances Vaughan.

Many other people helped in diverse ways. Sonja Hays provided superb secretarial and administrative assistance while working under intense time pressure. Jennifer Birkett helped release several writer's blocks.

The staffs of New Science Library and Shambhala Publications, especially my editor, Emily Hilburn, and Sally Furgeson were exceptionally friendly and supportive at all times. I am grateful to Samuel Bercholz, the editor-in-chief of Shambhala, for accepting this book and for backing it with his full support and resources. Under his guidance Shambhala has become one of the foremost publishing houses specifically committed to books addressing areas of social importance. And finally Ken Wilber, long a deeply cherished friend and inspiration, in his role as chief editor of New Science Library became also a deeply appreciated editor. To all these people and more I express my gratitude for their help in co-creating *Staying Alive*.

Clearly, the number one health issue for the planet is our very survival as a species.

—Richard Barnet

Only on the basis of an understanding of our behavior can we hope to control it in such a way as to ensure the survival of the human race.

—Senator William Fulbright

A PERSONAL PREFACE

Becoming Concerned

Each of us can remember experiences that moved us deeply, that shook the seemingly solid foundation of our lives, forced us to recognize how we had hidden from the truth, and told us in no uncertain terms that our old ways would no longer be enough. For me such a time came in 1981 during a trip to Asia.

I had gone to Thailand and Burma for several months. Although I had time to visit India beforehand, I decided not to: I had been told that if I stayed there I would probably get sick and might be unable to get to Burma on time. It sounds sensible enough, but think about what it really means! I was unwilling to visit a country with some 600 million people because I feared to live, even briefly, under the conditions that they have to accept from birth to death.

Even in Burma and Thailand there was still great suffering. The signs of needless poverty and disease were everywhere. Standing on a street corner for an hour I learned as much about diseases such as leprosy, congenital deformities, and tuberculosis of the spine as I had learned in medical school. In some cases I recognized diseases only from memories of old medical textbooks, since the illnesses had long since been vanquished in the West. The tragedy was that these diseases were treatable, if only adequate medical resources were available. Here they were not.

Everywhere the sheer numbers of people were extraordinary. To catch a bus in Rangoon sometimes meant hanging from the side while we tore through overcrowded streets and a cacophony of sound.

This was my introduction to Asia and my first taste of the conditions under which most of the world's population lives. Of course, there was also great joy and love in many people's lives. But the amount of preventable suffering was staggering. Overpopulation, poverty, malnutrition, pollution, disease; all were wreaking an extraordinary and unnecessary amount of pain.

Each day I spent some time sitting by a road watching the people who passed. As I did, the endless parade of people and their all-too-evident suffering pulled a prayer from me; a plea that I might use my life more wisely to help them and the countless millions like them.

"How could I have been so asleep?" I asked myself. Why hadn't I appreciated the conditions under which most of the world's people live? How could I have repressed the extent of preventable pain? Indeed, I had always considered myself quite knowledgeable about such things. But I was learning that there is a vast difference between a vague intellectual understanding of the world's problems, and directly experiencing them.

After two months I returned to the United States and experienced yet another culture shock. I had expected a sense of unfamiliarity. However, I was quite unprepared for the sense of unreality I felt pervading the busyness of daily lives and the enormous difficulty I experienced remembering what life is like for people in other parts of the world. So many activities seemed to be aimed at a continuous distraction away from deeper, more important concerns, and toward fostering what has rightly been called "tranquilization by the trivial."

What I was beginning to recognize were the ways in which cultures, and western cultures in particular, simply because of their greater affluence, function not only to uplift and ennoble us, but also to distract, trivialize, and deny. It has often been said that contemporary cultures function as vast conspiracies against contemplative living. Now I was beginning to appreciate that this conspiracy included not only philosophical and religious contemplation, but contemplation on the state of the world as well. Only by an active effort of will could I keep the living conditions of the world's poor in mind and hold intact the attitudes and decisions I had reached while exposed to them.

I felt an urgent need to understand global problems better and began reading about them. The more I read, the more appalled I became both at the vastness and urgency of our dilemmas and at my own ignorance of them. Increasing population, poverty, and pollution, decreasing resources, accelerating militarization, and spreading ecological imbalances quickly became blindingly obvious.

How could I not have recognized the true condition of our world?

"How could I have been so asleep?" I asked myself once again. Indeed, I had always considered myself quite knowledgeable about such things. But I was learning that there is a vast difference between a vague awareness that the world has problems and the precise knowledge of exactly how endangered it is.

Nor was I the only one asleep. My ignorance obviously reflected that of the culture. Very few people seemed to have any real appreciation of just what we were up against. In fact, only a few really wanted to know. We seemed to be latter-day Neros, fiddling and distracting ourselves in countless ways unavailable in Roman times, while our planet was polluted and plundered. I was beginning to appreciate the power of the psychological and social forces that keep us unconscious.

Shortly afterwards, New Year's Day, 1982 to be exact, I went to see the film *The Last Epidemic*, a vivid account by a group of physicians and scientists of the effects of nuclear war. I left in a state of shock. I had known nuclear war would be bad but had not appreciated just how incomprehensibly disastrous it would really be. Once again, the familiar questions swirled through my head. How could I have been so asleep? How could I not have recognized the true situation? How could I have thought I was knowledgeable and aware?

But in addition to the familiar questions there was something more. There was also a regret that I had this knowledge, because I knew that now I would have to start working on these issues. Part of me did not want to—I was already too busy—but I also knew that there was no turning back. Opening to that knowledge, experiencing the world's reality honestly demanded a response. Almost reluctantly I began to think about what I could do. Gradually, very gradually, as my understanding deepened, I began to see a crucial dimension that was being missed and where I might perhaps make a useful contribution.

For the more I reflected on our current crises, the more I recognized that they were all human-caused. To the extent they were human-caused, then to that extent their causes were to be sought in human behavior and in the psychological forces—the desires, defenses, phobias, and fantasies—that motivated that behavior. In other words, the roots of our dilemmas were largely psychological. The dilemmas themselves could therefore be seen as symptoms: global symptoms of our collective psychological disturbances.

If these psychological roots could be understood, then perhaps we could better understand the principles of skillful responses. The definition I like most describes an action as skillful to the extent that it reduces suffering and enhances well-being for everyone, including oneself. Psychology, then, might perhaps provide both novel and skillful insights.

Yet psychological causes and principles seemed to be very rarely recognized. Almost all discussions focused on economic, political, or military factors without any appreciation of the mental factors underlying them. The problems were seen as originating solely "out there" rather than both "out there" *and* "in here." The underlying sources—our minds—of both problems and solutions were usually overlooked. Much anger, blame, and attack were therefore directed out at the world, thereby often exacerbating the very emotions that had caused the problems in the first place. In other words, the failure to appreciate the psychological roots of our global situation appeared to reduce the depth and effectiveness of our responses and even render them counterproductive.

Here, then, was an entry point where a useful contribution might be made. For if one could demonstrate the centrality of psychological forces and develop a psychological analysis of the threats to human survival, then perhaps a psychology of human survival could be created. Perhaps a global psychology aimed at human survival was a strategic idea whose time had come. A small but growing number of mental health professionals seemed to be beginning to think along these lines so perhaps I could play a part.

As a first step I thought I would give some talks and see how people reacted. I therefore prepared a lecture that provided an overview of the global situation and included examples of practical insights from several schools of psychology. It seemed important to include several schools so as to avoid parochialism and to make it clear that we needed diverse approaches. In fact, we needed all the help we could get. It also seemed important to focus on insights that could be used to practical advantage in the world, rather than those that could merely be admired for their theoretical purity. It has been said that "philosophy leaves the world as it is." That may or may not be true, but there seemed no point in creating a psychology of human survival that left the world as it is, particularly since it might mean that there would soon be no world or psychology. Pragmatism had become a necessity.

I began by speaking to professional audiences and was delighted that most people's responses were positive. Given the facts about our situation, many people were moved and some began to play a more active role. Among mental health professionals at least, the ideas of a psychology of human survival seemed to make good sense. Each presentation reawakened in me a sense of both the urgency and the remarkable potential of our condition, so at least one of us was finding my talks helpful. This reawakening drew me deeper and deeper into the issues.

As it did, I became increasingly aware that the task facing us is twofold. One is to work to relieve the suffering in the world. The other is to work to relieve the psychological causes, starting first within ourselves, that contribute to this suffering. The challenge then, is not only to contribute but also to learn and mature in the process.

The more deeply I became involved, the more I felt pulled to begin writing about a psychology of human survival. In part, I felt inspired by a vision of what such a psychology might contribute and excited by the scope and purpose of the task. Then too, I really ached to see whether others would respond to the ideas that had gradually coalesced in my mind over the last two years.

But I also resisted taking on another task. I was already overdue on one book, and the idea of starting another made my hair curl. At this stage someone suggested finding a co-author who could do most of the actual writing if I presented an outline of the ideas.

As fate would have it, someone presented herself almost immediately; a very intelligent, competent, and psychologically sophisticated student who supported herself as a professional writer. Not only could she do it, she wanted to do it and headed off to the library to do background reading. Within a week she called back to quit. It was emotionally overwhelming, she said. The more she read, the more anxious she felt and the less she could sleep. I could certainly understand, and so we went our separate ways.

But the issues kept nagging at me, and finally I felt that they were too urgent to be ignored further. I laid aside my other work and began writing. For I felt that if people really appreciated the psychological roots of our current situation it might make a significant difference. How different cold war rhetoric might seem if the underlying mutual fear and paranoia were recognized, how unnecessary and counterproductive aspects of our current lifestyles might seem, how much we might learn about ourselves, and how much we and our planet might all benefit if we were to recognize the source of both our problems and our solutions where it truly is: within ourselves. It was with these hopes that I began writing.

• PART I •

THE STATE OF THE WORLD

1

INTRODUCTION

It is no secret that we have reached a critical time in our history, a time that may decide the fate of both our species and our planet.

It is a time of paradox. The evidence of human genius and inspiration is all around us; but so too is the evidence of ignorance and idiocy. On the one hand, we possess scientific, medical, and psychological resources undreamed of only decades ago. We have gone to the moon, fathomed the intricacies of the brain, and sent probes to the farthest reaches of the solar system. On the other hand, millions of people starve, our ecosystem is endangered, and nuclear arms threaten global suicide. In short, we possess unprecedented opportunities yet also face unprecedented threats.

Not surprisingly, this time of paradox has evoked many different interpretations. Some people focus on the positive aspects and predict an era of accelerating development and well-being.[1] Others feel awed by the enormity of our difficulties and predict nothing less than global catastrophe. Still others, appreciating both the opportunities and the dangers, see us facing an uncertain "developmental crisis of mankind"[2] whose outcome is ours to decide.[3] But whatever one's perspective, it is clear that our current age faces threats, challenges, opportunities, and choices of a kind, scope, and complexity never before encountered in human history.

Moreover, for the first time in millions of years of evolution, all the major threats to our survival are human-caused. Problems such as nuclear weapons, pollution, and ecological imbalance stem directly from our own behavior and can therefore be traced to psychological origins. This means that the current threats to human survival and well-being *are actually symptoms*, symptoms of our individual and shared mind set. The state of the world is therefore a creation and expression of our own minds, and it is to our minds that we must look for solutions. Of course, this is not to deny the importance of social, political, and economic forces, but simply to emphasize the underlying psychological causes.

Yet it is amazing how rarely these apparently obvious psychological factors are appreciated. While the good news is that growing numbers of people are mobilizing to respond to global dangers, the bad news is that most act without recognition of the psychological causes. What this means is that most interventions treat only symptoms rather than both symptoms and causes. The unfortunate result is often a suppression of symptoms rather than any real cure, since the underlying causes remain largely untouched.

This is similar to the situation that would exist if a therapist were to treat only the symptoms and complications of a psychological disturbance. For example, suppose an adolescent going through a developmental crisis of insecurity and defensiveness became aggressive and started attacking people. If the therapist tended only to their bruises, then the situation would probably recur. Even if the adolescent were punished or jailed, the underlying cause would remain untreated and might even be exacerbated. The aggression and its complications might be temporarily suppressed but would probably flare up again later. Only some type of therapy aimed at resolving the underlying developmental problems could be expected to be truly curative. The same principles hold true at the global level. If efforts to deal with nuclear weapons, for example, focus solely on establishing equal stockpiles then the underlying psychological forces that fuel the arms race remain untouched.

Therefore, to cure, or at least produce significant long-term improvement of global crises demands more than symptomatic treatment. It demands not just food for the starving and reduction of nuclear stockpiles, but also psychological understandings and contributions. Developing such understandings may be one of the most urgent tasks facing our generation and may determine the fate of all future generations.

Yet considering their importance it is amazing how little attention has been given to these psychological factors, even by mental health professionals. Of course, there have always been laudable exceptions, particularly in the area of war and international conflict. Albert Einstein, who was desperately concerned about human survival and who thought of war as a "savage and inhuman relic of an age of barbarism," was well aware of the importance of psychological forces. Some fifty years ago he wrote to Sigmund Freud that, "It would be of the greatest service to us all were you to present the problem of world peace in the light of your most recent discoveries, for such a presentation might well blaze the trail for new and fruitful modes of action."[4] Freud's response was typically pessimistic; he thought human beings were doomed to keep fighting. However, in recent years increasing numbers of more optimistic mental health professionals have begun searching for answers to Einstein's plea for "new and fruitful modes of action."

Yet to date, most psychological studies have been rather fragmentary. They tend to focus on only one particular problem, most often nuclear weapons, from one particular perspective, such as psychoanalysis. While these studies make valuable contributions, we also need a global psychology to address global threats and their psychological causes as a whole. This is the purpose of *Staying Alive*.

This book is therefore intended to provide both an overview of the threats as well as a framework with which to understand them.

In writing it, I have several goals in mind; goals which I believe are crucial for any psychological approach to human survival. These goals are:

1. To suggest the possibility of developing a global psychology of human survival that is not just a tidy theoretical abstraction but a practical working tool.

2. To provide a succinct overview of our current global difficulties so that people know precisely what we are up against.

3. To shift the perceived causes of our global dilemmas from exclusively "out there" in the world and other people to both "out there" *and* "in here" within us.

4. To mobilize and empower people. My hope is that once people are aware of the facts, these facts will pull them to respond and that these responses will be more effective because of the deeper understanding they express.

5. To help us use our current crises in a judo-like way for accelerated learning and growth. One of the major claims of this book is that our current crises, like all challenges, can be seen as opportunities; opportunities that may force us to mature rapidly, both as individuals and as cultures.

6. To show that all of us can make useful contributions to human survival.

7. To provide ideas that people will apply and test and then add to and improve so as to create a continuously growing and developing psychology of human survival.

These, then, are the results that I hope this book might help us achieve. With this aim in mind, the material is divided into four major sections that:

1. Outline the nature of the current global threats
2. Analyze their psychological causes
3. Deduce principles of effective response
4. Examine the psychological impact that the threats exert on us individually and collectively.

2

GLOBAL THREATS TO HUMAN SURVIVAL AND WELL-BEING

Because we have acted with only partial awareness we have upset the equilibrium and have torn the fabric of the universe, which now returns to exact its ecological reparation. Environmental degradation, alienation, urban decay, and social unrest are mirrors of the shortness of our vision of man and the universe. Our outer world reflects our inner conditions.

—*Duane Elgin*

Anyone who has read a newspaper in recent years is probably aware that we face not one but several global problems. Yet it is disturbing to find how very, very few people appreciate the extent and urgency of these crises.

This lack of knowledge probably reflects several factors. The first is the distressingly superficial coverage of international news by our media. But even when coverage is adequate, it can be very hard for us to really grasp the full implications of what we hear. Those of us living in developed countries have great difficulty appreciating the stark realities of life for the world's poverty-stricken majority, cushioned and protected from such experiences as we are.

Then, too, our ignorance also reflects psychological defense mechanisms. At times we simply do not want to let in the facts; it hurts too much. Consciously or unconsciously, we decide to shut down and remain ignorant rather than open ourselves to the full extent of suffering and tragedy that exist. Even psychologically sophisticated professionals may fall prey to these traps, since mental health professionals "like other people, want a predictable world and want to believe that the world is better managed than it really is. In fact, psychiatrists, as do others, engage in radical denial of problems beyond their influence."[1] In short, most of us, including the educated and psychologically sophisticated, remain relatively unaware of the true state of the world. Hence the following review of our global situation.

The purpose of presenting this review is certainly not to induce fear and guilt as is sometimes done, but rather to inform and motivate in a constructive way. Psychologists speak of the fusion of facts and values, suggesting that once the truth of a situation is recognized it evokes values and motives

5

appropriate to it.[2] "The truth will set you free," may not only be good theology but sound psychology as well, and once the facts of our current condition are fully appreciated, they too may evoke appropriate values and responses.

Fortunately, a number of detailed analyses of global trends have become available recently. Most of the following data are based on the best known of these, the *Global 2000 Report*, which was prepared at President Carter's request by the Council on Environmental Quality.[3] It must be emphasized that the following figures, though stark, are by no means sensationalistic. Rather, the *Global 2000 Report* concluded that, due to technical considerations, "Most of the study's quantitative results understate the severity of potential problems."[4]

This is *not* to say that the problems are unsolvable. Huge, complex, demanding, and urgent—yes, indeed! But unsolvable, no! Indeed, the very reason for writing this book is to argue that they are potentially solvable, and that psychological understanding may have a crucial role to play in their solution.

Deep psychological understanding involves not just theoretical knowledge of the world but also direct awareness of our own experience. It requires not just knowledge but also wisdom. Whereas knowledge is something we have, wisdom is something we are, and we develop it by reflecting on our personal experience. Therefore, it may be very useful to read the following account, not only to acquire information and facts, but also to observe your reactions to them. For these subjective reactions determine the nature of our actions and are therefore also vital to the psychology of human survival.

What, then, are the major threats to human survival and global well-being? Let us examine them under the headings of population, poverty, food, energy, environment, and nuclear weapons.

THE POPULATION BOMB

The rate of population growth is nothing less than staggering. It took humankind over a million years to reach a population of one billion in 1800 A.D. Yet today, only 185 years later, we number almost five billion, add yet another billion every thirteen years, and we will double our numbers in only forty years. This means that, even assuming projected increases in family planning, the world's population is expected to reach six billion by the year 2000 (less than fifteen years from now) and ten billion by 2030 (less than fifty years from now).[5]

Yet the National Academy of Sciences concluded that a world population of ten billion "is close to (if not above) the maximum that *an intensively managed world* might hope to support with some degree of comfort and individual choice."[6] Such an increase would demand producing more buildings, supplies, energy, and resources within the next fifty years than have been produced in all of human history. This is quite a task for a world that has not yet managed to supply adequately a population half that size. It is also why "the future of mankind is dependent upon being able to stem the population increase."[7]

The situation is further complicated by the fact that over 90 percent of this population growth will occur in less-developed countries. By the year 2000, some five billion people (80 percent of the world's populaton) will be packed into these already overcrowded areas.

POVERTY

This population explosion will exaggerate the already gaping disparities between the rich and the poor. At the present time, 2.5 billion people (over half the world's population) live in countries with average incomes of less than $500 per person. Of these people, one billion (one-fifth of the world's population) average less than $200 per year.[8] By contrast, per capita income in the developed countries is over $5,000, some thirty times greater than that of the poorest.[9]

Nor, unfortunately, are these inequities likely to change without drastic action. Rather, if current trends continue, it will be a case of the rich getting richer while the poor stay poor.

This poverty takes its toll in many, many forms. To mention but a few: 800 million people lack adequate housing or even shelter,[10] and over ten million suffer preventable blindness.[11] Safe, clean drinking water is only a dream in many countries, which means that epidemics such as hepatitis, typhoid, and parasites sweep through the population with tragic regularity. This tragedy is further complicated by the fact that over three billion people lack access to adequate health services.

These are extraordinary, even incomprehensible, figures, which convey very little of the suffering and desperation lying behind them. Nor do they give any sense of the vicious cycles that keep people trapped in poverty and disease. But with poverty comes sickness, inadequate health care, high death rates among children, and minimal educational and social resources. Sickness means inability to work and further poverty. Inadequate resources mean no retirement pay or pension and people who are dependent upon their children for support in old age. Because of the high child mortality rates, parents want large numbers of children to ensure that at least some will survive into adulthood. Hence the population continues to expand as a "result of the inhuman conditions under which these people live."[12] Minimal education cuts off escape into more skilled, better-paying jobs and means that vital information about such things as health care, contraception, and farming methods goes

7

unlearned. The result is a vicious cycle in which more and more people become more and more enmeshed. This is a far cry from the United Nations declaration (that all of us through our respective governments have signed) that says:

Everyone has the right to a standard of living which is adequate for the health and well-being of himself and of his family, including food, clothing, housing, and medical care and necessary social services, and the right to security in the event of unemployment, sickness, disability, widowhood, old age, or other lack of livelihood in circumstances beyond his control.

FOOD

Perhaps poverty's most devastating toll is taken by malnutrition and starvation. During the 1970s, the average person in the less-developed countries ate only 94 percent of the minimum amount of calories recommended by the United States Food and Drug Administration. At the present time, some fifteen to twenty million people die malnutrition-related deaths each year, and a further four to six hundred million people go malnourished. The Presidential Commission on World Hunger estimates that by the year 2000 their numbers will have swelled to an inconceivable 1.3 billion.[13]

One of the difficulties in discussing these issues is that the sheer enormity of the figures and of the suffering they symbolize is beyond our ability to grasp in any meaningful way. Only by a purposive act of will and imagination can we even begin to appreciate their true meaning because

We are deluged by facts but have lost or are losing our ability to *feel* them. The real defense of freedom is imagination, that feeling life of the mind that *actually* knows because it involves itself in its knowing.[14]

Imagine, then, for a moment, almost the entire population of California, Canada, or Czechoslovakia, or of every third person in England or France dying slowly, painfully, and preventably within a single year. Then imagine that scene repeated year after year after year, and imagine around every person who dies another thirty who are hungry and malnourished, and at last you have some sense of the true magnitude of suffering caused by hunger.

Yet awesome as it is, almost all predictions indicate that unless present political and economic priorities are drastically revised, the present situation will deteriorate. The next thirty years are expected to produce calamitous food drops in Asia, Africa, and the Middle East. If we do not reverse these trends we will witness famines on a scale unprecedented in human history, in which deaths will be counted in the hundreds of millions.[15]

Nobel Laureate Norman Borlaug, who was instrumental in introducing highly productive strains of crops to the Third World and is therefore sometimes called the father of "the green revolution," put it this way:

Expanding food production fast enough to meet the increasing needs of a large and growing population over the next four decades will be vital to the survival of civilization. In the next forty years alone, world food production must be upped by at least as much as it was increased during the entire 12,000-year period from the beginning of agriculture to the present day.[16]

This is a formidable project, to put it mildly.

ENERGY

While food shortages stalk much of the Third World, the resource shortage most familiar in the developed countries is energy. The oil embargo in the 1970s shocked us in a way no studies or warnings had managed. Yet the long-term effects on our lifestyles and economies have been mild. As yet they amount to little more than inconveniences, and supplies, though more costly, are once again adequate. Consequently, there has been little motivation for conservation and a switch to renewable energy sources such as solar, wind, and hydroelectric power. While some gains have been made, they are considerably less than they might have been.[17] The result is that the western world continues to squander precious nonrenewable energy resources, remains vulnerable to embargoes, and has yet to come to terms with the looming reality of dwindling supplies.

The situation is very different, however, in less developed countries. There the impact of rising energy prices has been dramatic and sometimes devastating. Desperately needed finances have been diverted toward payment for energy resources, thus reducing the money available for raising living standards and providing essential services.[18]

Moreover, the dramatic increases in global food production during the 1950s to 1970s and the projected increases through the remainder of this century are heavily dependent on petroleum and petroleum-related products. This threatens the so-called "green revolution" and suggests that food prices will increase significantly in coming years.[19]

ENVIRONMENTAL CONSEQUENCES

The dramatic changes in world population, resource utilization, and energy consumption obviously hold major implications for the environment, and "virtually every aspect of the earth's ecosystems and resource base will be affected."[20] These include the amount of farmable land, drinkable water, and deserts; the atmosphere and climate; forest and vegetation patterns; and species survival. But the *Global 2000 Report* concluded that "perhaps the most serious environmental development will be an accelerating deterioration and loss of the resources essential for agriculture."[21]

AGRICULTURE

Much of the world's farmlands are already being pushed to their production limits and beyond. When these pressures are combined with poor management and lack of fertilizers, the inevitable result is a sorry state of soil depletion. If current trends continue—as they surely will without a major shift in global priorities—then the world's farmlands will show significant deterioration by the turn of the century. Such factors as erosion, nutrient loss, pollution, and water shortages are expected to reduce productivity, destroy farmlands, and increase deserts.

Conservative estimates predict an expansion of the world's deserts by some 20 percent by the year 2000. In addition, the United Nations has identified almost eight million square miles of land where the risk of desertification is rated as "high" or "very high." This huge area is some two and a half times the size of the world's current deserts. What this means is that unless we exercise considerably more care than we have up until now, we will end up losing an irreplaceable resource the size of Europe and the United States combined.

The world's forests are also under severe pressure and, if current trends continue, may be largely depleted early next century. Deforestation is already producing a variety of unfortunate effects that demonstrate the complex interactions that can occur between resources, consumption patterns and ecology.[22]

For example, in less-developed countries most wood is used for cooking fuel. Yet increasing population pressures and decreasing wood availability have created a shift toward the burning of dung and crop wastes. This deprives the soil of nutrients, and by reducing its organic content degrades the soil's ability to hold moisture. Yet for the world's poor, these organic materials are usually the only source of nutrients available to maintain farmland productivity, and the green revolution's high-yield grain crops are heavily dependent on high nutrient levels. The net effect is therefore a tragic downward spiral of environmental degradation and resource depletion at a time when food demands are rapidly increasing.[23]

ATMOSPHERE AND CLIMATE

All of us are familiar to some extent with the effects of atmospheric pollution. Urban air pollution is well recognized, but phenomena such as acid rain and rising carbon dioxide concentrations are likely to be far greater long-term problems.

"A chemical leprosy is eating into the face of North America and Europe. This chemical legacy is commonly called acid rain."[24] Acid rain occurs when sulphur and nitrogen oxide emissions combine with atmospheric water vapor to form acid. Its effects are not fully understood but probably include damage to lakes, forests, soils, crops, and buildings throughout much of Europe and Northeast America.

Deforestation and the use of fossil fuels also result in increased atmospheric levels of carbon dioxide.[25] By the year 2000, atmospheric carbon dioxide will be approximately one-third greater than pre-industrial levels and could double within some fifty or sixty years. Such a rapid increase, quite unprecedented in human history, is expected to alter global temperature, climate, and agriculture. Even a rise of one degree centigrade in average global temperatures, a shift considerably less than anticipated, would result in significant polar ice cap melting and a warmer climate than at any time during the last 1,000 years.[26]

CONCLUSIONS

What these and many other facts make clear is that we are in a phase of unprecedented ecological disruption and "drawdown"; a phase in which we are consuming the planet's resources faster than they are being replaced. We may have inherited the world from our forefathers, but we are now also borrowing it from our children. Not only does untold suffering from preventable causes such as poverty and starvation exist now, but also we are setting the stage for drastically greater suffering in the future.

We are, in short, mortgaging our future and that of future generations. For as ecological systems are disrupted, resources depleted, and populations expanded, correction becomes increasingly difficult with every year. Each decade before zero population growth is established means another half billion people requiring food, shelter, and supplies.[27] Likewise, restoring deserts may take decades *after* population pressures are removed.

Yet as Erik Dammann points out in his book, *The Future in Our Hands*, which launched an international campaign of the same name:

The world is not threatened by catastrophe in the future. The greater part of mankind is already experiencing catastrophe today. None of us would talk in terms of *future* catastrophe if our present family income amounted to less than one dollar a day, if we lived with our family in a hut or shack without water or electricity, if we were starving and lost every second child which was born, if our surviving children were physically or mentally destroyed by deficiency diseases, if there were no doctors available. If we lived like this, it would be per-

11

fectly clear that catastrophe was already an accomplished fact. This is the way humanity lives today. Not distant, small groups. *Mankind* is living like this. The majority of us.[28]

These are the facts we must be willing to recognize if we are to respond appropriately. On our willingness to recognize them hangs the fate of the earth.

3

THE NUCLEAR SHADOW

The splitting of the atom has changed everything save our mode of thinking, and thus we drift toward unparalleled catastrophe.

—Albert Einstein

Most of us fortunate enough to live in developed countries have not yet had to confront personally the problems discussed so far. Though this situation may soon change, for us the most pressing concern is the nuclear issue. For with the spread of nuclear weapons, the survival, not just of individuals and cultures, but of all civilization, is at stake. The nuclear shadow hangs over each and every one of us as probably the most encompassing and urgent threat in human history. Humankind is now on trial, a trial we ourselves have created, and if we find each other guilty, the penalty we exact will be death.

AMOUNT OF NUCLEAR WEAPONS

In the 1960s, the American Secretary of Defense Robert McNamara suggested that the United States needed approximately 200 nuclear warheads. With that number, he argued, the United States could destroy one-third of the Russian population and two-thirds of their industry, thereby eradicating the Soviet Union as a major industrial power and wreaking on it greater havoc than any disaster in history. Today the United States constructs 200 warheads every two months and possesses a total of some 30,000. Worldwide there exist some 50,000,[1] and today will see the construction of several more.

The total explosive power of these weapons amounts to some twenty billion tons of TNT.[2] Such an amount is so large as to be almost incomprehensible. However, it becomes disconcertingly graphic when it is realized that a freight train carrying it would stretch for approximately *four million miles.* Twenty billion tons of TNT, in other words, would fill a train that could circle the earth 160 times, or extend to the moon *and back* eight times. It represents an explosive power 1.6 million times that of the Hiroshima bomb, which was, at least by today's standards, a mere squib of 12.5 kilotons, yet was sufficient to destroy a city and kill 130,000 people. Likewise, twenty billion tons of TNT dwarf into insignificance the three million tons of all the bombs dropped during World War II. All the explosive power of all the weapons from all the wars waged throughout human history would not amount to more than a fraction of the power of one of today's larger warheads.

THE RISK OF ACCIDENTS

Needless to say, these awesome weapons are controlled and guarded by some of the most sophisticated and complex security systems ever devised. Yet that very complexity renders them susceptible to error, both human and mechanical,[3] and results in a "randomly self-activating system."[4] Thus, for example, the North American Radar Air Defense System (NORAD), designed to detect nuclear attack, had 151 false alarms labeled "serious" and 3,703 lesser alarms in the eighteen months preceding June 30, 1980.[5] Presumably similar errors have occurred in the Soviet system, perhaps even more since their computers are generally regarded as less sophisticated than American ones. These errors must be diagnosed in less than the thirty minutes it takes for intercontinental missiles to reach their targets, or even the six to ten minutes required for submarine-launched weapons.

These dangerously short reaction times have created pressures for the introduction of "launch-on-warning systems." These are tactics designed to avoid the loss of one's missiles by launching them almost immediately, in some plans within seven minutes, after an apparent attack is detected.[6] This speed of response is purchased, however, at the cost of still further automation and dependency on computers and still less time for the detection of errors. Human decision-making in such a system is minimized. In military jargon, "they take the humans out of the loop." One United States Congressman's response sums up the danger: "I fear this may take the human out of the planet."[7]

Military commanders argue quite justifiably that they have taken enormous precautions and that the risks of accidental launch are minimal. However, it is hard to feel completely reassured, given the enormous talent of both humans and computers for error, and the fact that a single error might be our last.

The bombs themselves have also been subject to accident and error. In addition to having been misplaced and lost, bombs have fallen out of planes with disturbing regularity. In 1961 a plane carrying a twenty-four-megaton weapon (approximately 2,000 times larger than the Hiroshima bomb) crashed in North Carolina. Fortunately for us, that bomb had six safety mechanisms, and even more fortunately, only five of them failed. Other nuclear weapons lost from planes and submarines, both American and Soviet, have never been found.[8]

EFFECTS OF BUILDING NUCLEAR WEAPONS

But even if these weapons never explode, either deliberately or accidentally, their very construction entails risks. At the present time, not a single site exists for the permanent storage of radioactive material.[9] In the United States alone there are now over seventy million gallons of highly concentrated, highly radioactive waste and thousands upon thousands of tons of less active material.[10] This amount is expected to double in twenty-five years, yet to date a possible site for permanent storage has not even been identified.[11]

Just how critical these concerns are becomes starkly apparent when it is remembered that some of these substances are among the most toxic known and may have half-lives extending over hundreds or even thousands of years. For example, plutonium has a half-life of 24,000 years, is concentrated in the food chain, and can cause cancer in a dose of approximately one microgram. Yet it takes some five to ten *kilograms*, about a billion times the cancer-causing dose, to make a small nuclear weapon, and a nuclear reactor produces tens or hundreds of kilograms of it per year. We are faced, therefore, with finding ways of permanently storing substances that are likely to remain toxic for periods longer than civilization has existed.

THE WASTE OF RESOURCES

Yet even if these weapons are never exploded and waste storage problems are solved, there still remains the problem of the enormous waste of resources, money, and manpower. Nuclear weapons now consume $100 billion per year worldwide. In 1983 total military expenditures consumed an inconceivable $660 billion, an amount equivalent to $1.8 billion per day or $1.25 million per minute, and the amount continues to rise each year.[12] As Bernard Lown, President of International Physicians for the Prevention of Nuclear War, notes, "A small fraction of these expenditures could provide the world with adequate food and sanitary water supply, housing, education, and modern health care."[13] Indeed, the Presidential Commission on World Hunger estimated that it would cost only $6 billion per year to eradicate malnutrition, an amount equivalent to less than four days' arms expenditure.[14] Pope Paul IV anguished that the arms race kills whether the weapons are used or not, and President Eisenhower lamented that "every gun that is made, every warship launched, every rocket fired, signifies in the final sense a theft from those who hunger and are not fed, and those who are cold and not clothed. The world in arms is not spending money alone. It is spending the sweat of its laborers, the genius of its scientists, the hopes of its children."[15]

Although the world has been tragically slow to realize the fact, wars over resources may now be anachronistic since the same monies spent on technology for the benefit of all could provide sufficiently for all.[16]

EFFECTS OF NUCLEAR WAR

And if nuclear weapons were used? The effects predicted for even relatively small-scale nuclear wars are so awesome, devastating, and complex that I can not hope to do justice to them here. Indeed, even nuclear scientists and policy makers have repeatedly underestimated the complications of nuclear explosions. Every few years brings yet another newly recognized problem,[17] and it is becoming apparent that "the short-term effects that are relatively easy to quantify—fire, blast, and radioactive contamination—may be matched or even vastly overshadowed by longer-term, less-predictable environmental effects."[18] "The consequences would go so far beyond all our human experience as to be totally unpredictable. . . . We can be sure only that it would transcend any calamity that the world has experienced."[19]

For example, a single twenty-megaton explosion on New York City would be more devastating than any single catastrophe in human history. However, its effects are still predictable: e.g., fallout covering tens of thousands of square miles and an estimated twenty million people dead (10 percent of the United States population).[20] But the effects of some ten or twenty thousand or more explosions are quite incomprehensible, though immediate global effects would include pollution by nitrogen oxides, dust, smoke, and hundreds of radioactive substances.[21]

Atmospheric pollution from dust and smoke would result in a darkened world in the throes of a "nuclear winter." Reduced sunlight could lower global temperatures to below freezing even if "only" 100 megatons (less than 1 percent of the superpower arsenals) were exploded.[22]

The ozone layer would also be at risk. The National Academy of Sciences concluded that exploding less than half the superpowers' weapons would destroy some 70 percent of atmospheric ozone in the northern hemisphere.[23] Yet ozone is crucial for life because it filters and protects us from the harmful effects of the sun's ultraviolet rays. Destroying 70 percent of it would mean that two to five minutes' exposure to sunlight would produce blindness, and ten minutes would produce severe incapacitating sunburn. Though it would disappear in days, ozone restoration could require decades. Facts such as these suggest that much civil defense planning, including the rapid movement of tens of millions of people to "safe areas," is largely based on ignorance or fantasy.[24]

The expected biological consequences of nuclear war are, to say the least, severe. Animals and people would be irradiated, blinded, polluted, and frozen; plants and crops largely destroyed. The photosynthesis of surviving plants would be greatly reduced, and "agriculture as we know it would then, for all practical purposes, have come to an end."[25]

The implications for humankind of these incomprehensible dislocations have been summarized by both Soviet and American leaders. In the words of

16

a Soviet government publication, "Nuclear war would be a universal disaster, and it would probably mean the end of civilization. It may lead to the destruction of all mankind." "The survivors, if any," said President Carter, "would live in despair among the poisoned ruins of a civilization that has committed suicide."[26]

In short, nuclear war, even of the most limited type, would result in devastation and suffering on a scale quite unknown in human history. A full-scale conflict would mean the death of billions and could quite possibly spell the extinction of our species.

But though current weapons may be capable of ensuring our extinction, the arms race continues unabated. While both conventional and nuclear weapon stockpiles are being further expanded, a whole new generation of weapons is on the drawing board, together with plans for stationing some of them in space. "In the absence of meaningful negotiations between the United States and the Soviet Union," says United States Senator Larry Pressler, "the first phase of 'star wars' could develop at any time."[27] Indeed, "the issue of weapons in space brings mankind to a threshold no less significant than the one we faced in the forties, when the atom bomb was invented."[28] Anti-satellite missiles, particle beam weapons, laser firing "fortresses in the sky," and more are currently being designed.[29] The arms race continues to accelerate in an ever more costly, deadly, and insane spiral with no end in sight.

OUR WORLD IN SUMMARY

These, then, are the major issues confronting humankind today. Together we stand at an historical crossroads where trends that have been gathering momentum across decades and even centuries are colliding in ways that can be denied and ignored only at the cost of untold sickness, starvation, suffering, death, and perhaps even omnicide.

Most of these problems, by their very nature, are not amenable to quick fixes and are interpenetrated by complex social, economic, and political forces. New levels of cooperative planning and commitment are required if we are to escape the consequences of current trends and to avoid incomprehensible amounts of human suffering. The Council on Environmental Quality therefore concluded:

The problems of preserving the carrying capacity of the earth and sustaining
the possibility of a decent life for human beings that inhabit it are enormous
and close upon us. . . . The time for action . . . is running out. Unless nations
collectively and individually take bold and imaginative steps towards im-
proved social and economic conditions, reduced fertility, better management
of resources, and the protection of the environment, the world must expect a
troubled entry into the twenty-first century.[30]

On our willingness to examine these problems and ourselves, and to work toward resolving both the problems and the psychological forces within us that created them, hangs our fate. Let us therefore begin by turning to an examination of the psychological forces within us and between us that have led to this situation and those that may yet lead us out of it. Let us then ask these questions of our current threats:

1. What are their psychological causes?
2. What are the psychological principles underlying skillful responses?
3. What psychological effects do these threats exert on us, both individually and collectively?

• PART 2 •

THE STATE OF OUR MINDS

4

THE PSYCHOLOGICAL ORIGINS
OF OUR DILEMMA

*In my opinion it is Man's Temperament that decides his fate. There is no other
kind of fate. I do not believe therefore that he must necessarily continue to follow
the path which leads only downwards; he may yet turn about before he arrives at
the very end.*

—Albert Schweitzer

Since all the major threats to human survival and well-being are human-
caused, they are, of course, deeply, though not exclusively, psychological in
origin. The state of the world, then, is a reflection of the state of our individual
and collective minds. From this perspective, our "problems" are actually
"symptoms," and to understand their cause and cure we must understand
ourselves and our behavior.

To obtain this understanding we need to avoid grasping at dogmatic,
overly simple answers. We are, at the very least, awesomely complex creatures
and so are the problems we have created. It is therefore not particularly helpful to try to explain the state of the world solely in terms of one's favorite
scapegoat, whether it be Russian paranoia, faulty childrearing, or material-
istic decadence.

All behavior is the result of many causes. To attribute it to only one or a
few of these causes is therefore to lose breadth, power, and flexibility in both
understanding and response.* Therefore, it will be important for us to draw
on a variety of psychological schools and approaches since each school tends
to focus on one particular type of cause.

Let us then attempt to ground our global psychology, not in any one
school, belief, or perspective, but rather within an open-minded, inclusive
framework that acknowledges the possible value and complementarity of
many approaches. In doing so, we are doing at the psychological level what we
are attempting at the international; namely, to set aside traditional boundaries

---

*This tendency of trying to account for complex phenomena by only one or a few factors is
called "extravagance" by psychologists and "degeneracy" by mathematicians.

and conflicts and to welcome for objective appraisal the potential contributions of all schools—behavioral and psychodynamic, individual and social, cognitive and existential, Eastern and Western.

Each of these schools provides a particular view of human nature and pathology that can be extended to an analysis of the threats to human survival and well-being. For example, cognitive psychology suggests the importance of beliefs, assumptions, and ignorance; behaviorism reminds us of the importance of inappropriate reinforcers; psychoanalysis makes distressingly clear the powerful role of defense mechanisms; the humanistic, existential, and transpersonal traditions point to the costs of inauthentic living and failed actualization; and the Eastern traditions point to the devastating effects of addiction, aversion, and delusion.

Each of these approaches has contributions to make. Perhaps the crucial question is: "Which insights are most practically useful, which will allow us to most effectively understand and deal with the situations?" The criterion here is a simple, pragmatic one.

The following, then, is an overview of strategic psychological factors that may help us understand current global difficulties and point to appropriate responses.

The major dimensions examined include:

1. The cognitive factors of thoughts, beliefs, and assumptions
2. Behaviorism and reinforcement
3. Social learning and the media
4. "The three poisons": addiction, aversion, and delusion
5. Perceptual tendencies of dualism and fragmentation
6. Defense mechanisms
7. Fear
8. Immaturity and inauthenticity, both individual and social.

5

THOUGHTS, BELIEFS, AND ASSUMPTIONS

---

*There is no more self-contradictory concept
than that of "idle thoughts."
What gives rise to the perception of a whole world
can hardly be called idle.
Every thought you have
contributes to truth or to illusion.*

—*Anonymous*

Within recent years there has been a growing recognition of the awesome power of thoughts and beliefs to shape our experience and behavior. Thoughts and beliefs determine what we look for, what we recognize, and how we interpret what we recognize. What is crucial about these processes is that they tend to be self-fulfilling and self-prophetic.

That is, beliefs tend to argue for their own validity since they shape perception and behavior in self-consistent ways.[1] For example, if I believe that all French people are angry and hostile I will tend to be particularly sensitive to any anger they display and may even act in ways which elicit it from them. In other words, our beliefs lead us to perceive those things that tell us that the beliefs are correct.

Unfortunately, the dangers of this process are compounded by the fact that most of it operates unconsciously.[2] We do not even notice how our perception is being biased. Therefore, we tend to mistake our beliefs, which are statements about reality, for reality. Rather than recognizing our beliefs they tend to determine what we recognize. Consequently, "there is nothing more difficult than to become critically aware of the presuppositions of one's own thoughts . . . every thought can be scrutinized directly except the thought by which we scrutinize."[3]

But become aware of our presuppositions we must. For only then can we recognize the destructive beliefs creating our contemporary crises. We can divide these into categories of:

1. Beliefs about ourselves
2. Beliefs about beliefs

3. Beliefs about others
4. Beliefs about the world, weapons, and warfare

The following may be particularly crucial.

Beliefs About Ourselves

Every decision you make stems from what you think you are,
and represents the value that you put upon yourself.

Anonymous

While all beliefs are powerful, those we hold about ourselves are especially so. When we believe something about ourselves we make it part of ourselves. For our self-image, what we think we are, is a construction of our
beliefs. These beliefs are selected on the basis of our past, but they themselves
select our future, telling us not only what we are but also what we can and
cannot become.

All that we say, think, or do is therefore a function of our beliefs about
ourselves. Together they construct our identity, our potential, and our prison
of self-imposed limits. But we do not have to accept them as dictators and
limits of our worth and capacity. Rather, we can exchange them for ones that
are more fulfilling and empowering. Small wonder then that so much of psychotherapy and psychological growth consists of learning to recognize limiting self beliefs for what they are, simply beliefs.

Self beliefs that are particularly important with regard to our world situation include those that limit our sense of power and effectiveness. "There is
nothing I can do," is the classic statement of impotence. Other power problems begin with, "I can't . . .," "I could never . . .," "I'm not qualified to . . .,"
or, "No one would listen to me." One whole class of limiting beliefs takes the
general form of, "I'm too _____." (Fill in the blank with your favorite, e.g.,
young/old, scared/angry, fat/thin, etc.). The apathy and inaction that these
beliefs create can then be rationalized by that all-time favorite, "It's not my
responsibility."

Beliefs About Beliefs

Faulty beliefs about beliefs can be downright dangerous. When people forget
that their ideologies and political systems are beliefs and mistake them for
"the truth," then they become willing to fight, kill, and die for them. This
situation becomes even more dangerous when people forget that any belief is
necessarily limited and only a partial statement of the truth. They then make
claims that their beliefs are not only the truth, but the whole truth and the
only truth. Inquisitions, executions, and wars get started, rationalized, and
glorified in this way.

Even though a belief system is intrinsically beneficial, it can become a source of conflict when people believe it is the only truth and that other views are necessarily wrong or evil. For example, the world's great religions contain some of the most inspiring and ennobling of all human ideas, yet Hindus, Muslims, Christians, and Jews have fought for centuries over claims to exclusive truth. Likewise, capitalism has brought enormous material benefits to many people. However, those who believe it to be the only truth have sometimes trampled on people experimenting with other ways.

Beliefs About Others

Beliefs about others and our relationships to them are also crucial. Particularly dangerous here are beliefs that blame others, dehumanize them, or see them as fundamentally inferior to ourselves. Obvious examples here include, "It's their fault that they're hungry," "They are to blame for the arms race," "'They' are different from 'us,'" "You can't trust them," and, in the extreme case, "They're not really human."

Unfortunately, some of the most extreme examples come from Soviet and American leaders. They describe each other with tragic regularity as, for example, "Godless monsters,"[4] "the focus of evil in the modern world," or as unwilling to maintain even "elementary norms of decency."[5] When leaders hold beliefs such as these about each other the chances for meaningful dialogue are, obviously, perilously slim.

Beliefs that view relationships from a competitive "us versus them" perspective are particularly likely to arouse hostility and aggression. This becomes particularly dangerous when it is believed that the relationship is one in which whatever one side gains, the other must lose.* In its most extreme form this becomes the belief that only one side can survive.

Such beliefs lead to a variety of destructive social processes, and the current hostility between the superpowers presents a tragic example. People on both sides tend to believe that Marxism and capitalism are locked in an inexorable struggle for survival and world domination. "The march of freedom and democracy . . . will leave Marxism-Leninism on the ash heap of history," claims President Reagan; "Nuclear war is being planned by the apostles of the arms race . . . with the cold-blooded composure of gravediggers," say the Soviets.[6] This type of belief system represents an example of a full-blown Manichaean world view; a view in which the earth is seen as a battleground

---

*Technically this is known as a "zero-sum game" because the total of gains and losses adds up to zero. "Variable-sum games," on the other hand, are not limited in this way and so one side can gain without the other having to lose and in some cases both sides may gain together. Zero-sum games tend to make for competition and hostility; variable-sum games for neutrality or cooperation. Whether we and national leaders believe relationships, and particularly international relationships, are zero-sum or variable-sum is therefore vitally important to the way we approach them.

on which the forces of light (us) are locked in mortal combat with the forces of darkness (them).

Such beliefs are both cause and effect of a variety of malignant social processes. These include suspiciousness, hostility, a focus on differences and a denial of commonalities, a belief that solutions can be obtained only by domination, and a temptation to resort to coercion and deception. Once such processes are set in motion, they tend to elicit the very hostility which was feared. The result is that they tend to "prove" the apparent validity of the beliefs that created them as well as the "wisdom" and "foresight" of those who held them. The self-prophetic power of beliefs is thereby demonstrated once again.

Beliefs About Weapons, War, and the World

There are also dangerous yet usually unquestioned assumptions about defense and warfare. For example, since less than one week of each year's arms expenditure could eradicate world starvation, there is the question as to whether we really believe it is worthwhile to allow hundreds of millions of people to starve to death in order to arm ourselves.

Numerous other questionable beliefs underlie current nuclear strategies. Those related to the size of nuclear stockpiles include the ideas that, "It is unrealistic to think that nuclear weapons can be reduced or eliminated," that "Nuclear superiority is possible," and that "More weapons provide more security." Other potentially suicidal ideas about nuclear war include the beliefs that "Limited nuclear wars can be fought without erupting into full-scale conflicts," and "Nuclear war is winnable."[7]

Questionable beliefs about the world are also rampant. Beliefs such as "It's hopeless," and "There is nothing that can be done," though quite understandable in view of the enormity of our difficulties, may exacerbate apathy and despair and prove dangerously self-fulfilling. Likewise, beliefs that "There is not enough food to go around," or that "There's no way of getting the food to people" are not only patently incorrect, they are dangerous.[8]

As is obvious, many of these beliefs are questionable at best and frequently contradictory. Such contradictions are usually obliterated from awareness by psychological defense mechanisms. Unfortunately, these same defense mechanisms also obliterate an accurate view of the world, and of appropriate responses to it. For if we are unwilling to look honestly at our beliefs we cannot afford to look honestly at the world and risk seeing that things are not as we believe. We will examine these defense mechanisms shortly, but first let us examine the contributions of behavior modification.

6

REINFORCEMENT AND SOCIAL LEARNING

Many of the same conditions that produce today's greatest perils also open fascinating new potentials.

—Alvin Toffler

REINFORCERS

For the behaviorist, behavior can be understood primarily in terms of reinforcement. What we are reinforced for we tend to do; what we are punished for we tend not to do. From this apparently simplistic formula, behaviorists have been able, through a careful analysis of the effects of different types of reinforcement, to construct a remarkably precise and experimentally validated account of environmental effects on behavior. Let us then examine the way in which the principles they have uncovered may account for our current global difficulties.

Our individual and international behaviors represent choices based on expected rewards or reinforcement. It follows, therefore, that our current difficulties should be traceable to inappropriate social, economic, and political reinforcement patterns. These patterns are, of course, incredibly complex, but we can recognize several trends that appear to have shaped societal and international reinforcers in dangerous directions.

One obvious factor involves the different potency of immediate as opposed to delayed gratification. As common sense tells us and behaviorists document, reinforcement is far more potent when it is immediate rather than when it is delayed.[1] This difference is particularly important because we are now dealing with longer-term consequences than ever before.

For example, many of the difficulties we face have long lag periods before their effects become identifiable. Thus, pollution can take years to accumulate to toxic threshold levels, years more before diseases or ecological imbalances are recognized, and decades before cause-and-effect relationships are identified. Likewise, the squandering of precious nonrenewable resources may not result in significant depletion for many years. Similarly, it may be decades before forests are depleted, fertile earth reduced to desert, or before radioactive wastes outstrip temporary storage sites or result in serious accidents.

Yet at the same time that we are dealing with longer-range consequences than ever before, we are also reinforcing ourselves and our political leaders for ensuring primarily short-term gratification. For example, few politicians have been willing to support the legislation necessary to reduce consumption of nonrenewable fuels. For most of them the immediate personal consequences of possible nonreelection far outweigh the long-term widespread consequences of resource depletion, pollution, and economic disruption. In other words, the consequences of our current decisions may not be felt for years, decades, or even generations after politicians have left office, governments have fallen, or we ourselves have moved from the areas we polluted, depleted, or contaminated.

In addition, leaders are often geographically and emotionally distanced from the consequences of their decisions. For example, leaders can now start wars while living safely in bunkers located hundreds or even thousands of miles from the conflict, can merely push buttons rather than engage in hand-to-hand combat, can allow millions to starve without ever setting eyes on a hungry person, or can pass legislation allowing massive pollution or ecological disturbance while living in air-conditioned comfort.

In summary, today's large, complex societies frequently act to separate decision makers from the consequences of their decisions. To use the language of sociologists, we appear to have moved in the direction of low-synergy cultures.[2] The degree of synergy is determined by the extent to which a person's decisions benefit both self and others simultaneously. The lower the synergy in the culture, the greater the conflict.

If we consider the planet as a whole and the nations as individuals in its global culture, then it is apparent that this global culture is also one of low synergy. Individual nation states function largely as laws unto themselves and are reinforced for dominating resources and one another.

Current social and economic systems also reinforce many behaviors that enhance international problems.[3] Armaments are one such system. The arms business is extraordinarily lucrative, amounting to some $25 to $35 billion per year of international trade,[4] playing a major role in the balance of payments of some countries, and employing half of the scientists and engineers in the United States and one-half million worldwide.[5] The economic and social status of millions therefore hinges on the perpetuation and continuous expansion of arms production and sales. Without the provision of adequate alternate employment millions continue to have a vested interest in a world that ever continues to arm itself.

Though this discussion has emphasized the factors reinforcing those in power, these factors are closely linked to citizen choices. Each of our individual lifestyle and reinforcement choices is part of a complex chain of reinforcements that selectively supports similar social and political choices.[6] For example, our choice to drive cars rather than to use public transportation results in greater gasoline demands, which in turn reinforces suppliers and poli-

ticians for increasing immediate supplies even at the cost of long-term depletion. "We blame the politicians," says Erik Dammann, "without understanding that they are merely acting in accordance with our own attitudes about
values and goals."[7]

SOCIAL LEARNING

As their field evolved, certain behavior modifiers came to appreciate the exceptional importance of social factors in learning and also to understand that
not all learning could be accounted for simply by reinforcement alone. From
this came an appreciation of the importance of modeling. Humans are natural
imitators, and we learn from what others model or demonstrate to us. We
tend to mimic what we see others doing, and particularly what we see others
being rewarded for doing.

These people we imitate need not even be present. Simply reading about
them or watching them on television can be sufficient. In fact, the media provide types and intensities of modeling to which we would otherwise never be
exposed. Social learning theorists have therefore become increasingly interested in the effects of the media, and a considerable amount of research data is
available.

Media impact is a complex issue fraught with emotional charges and
countercharges. But emotionalism aside, there seems little question that the
media in general and television in particular exert enormous and growing
psychological and social effects. In the United States, children spend more
time in front of a television than in front of a schoolteacher,[8] and two-thirds
of the population gets most of its news from television. A survey of some 500
"leading Americans" concluded that "television was thought to be the most
influential institution in the United States . . . more powerful than the President or Congress or the U. S. Supreme Court in its ability to influence the
perceptions and actions of our country."[9]

This influence has become an issue of increasing concern for mental
health professionals who have now conducted over 3,000 research studies.[10]
Their conclusions are dramatic. As had been suspected, television does indeed
affect the intellectual and emotional development of children. However, it
may also produce psychological and behavioral changes in people of all ages.

While most research has focused on television's effects on individuals, the
broader social and global issues also beg for attention, and have finally begun
to receive it.[11] Knowing the power of modeling in general and television
modeling in particular, it is hard not to be deeply concerned by current media
programming. A single evening's viewing makes disturbingly clear the preoccupation with violence and warfare, the glorification of aggressive and con-
sumptive lifestyles, the reliance on sensationalism and emotionalism, and the
avoidance of deeper analyses of complex controversial issues.

Though laudable exceptions exist, most television programs make no

29

attempt to present adequately the urgency and complexity of current global issues. Rather, the media seem to function largely as a distracting and trivializing "cultural barbiturate," narcotizing us into indifference and unconsciousness, and encouraging patterns of buying and consumption that exacerbate the problems they ignore. Our success in addressing the major issues of our time may well depend on the extent to which the mass media become agents of thoughtful education, analysis, and "consciousness raising" rather than continuing as agents of distraction and denial as they are now.[12]

7
VIEWS FROM THE EAST

The history of science is rich in the example of the fruitfulness of bringing two sets of techniques, two sets of ideas, developed in separate contexts for the pursuit of truth, in contact with each other.

—*Robert Oppenheimer*

Until very recently, Westerners usually assumed that our own psychologies were the only ones worthy of serious consideration, and that those of other cultures amounted to little more than primitive superstitions. Indeed, our attitude has been uncomfortably similar to that of one of the early British envoys to India. He made himself famous, or infamous, by announcing that he had never felt the need to learn the native language because he knew the Indians had nothing worthwhile to say.

However, within recent years the extent of our hubris has become increasingly apparent. It is clear that we have underestimated the sophistication of certain Eastern psychologies.[1] Certainly they suggest several valuable insights for a psychology of human survival. Taking Buddhist psychology as an example, we find that it offers sophisticated analyses of many causes of individual and social pathology. However, classical Buddhism claims that all these causes can be traced to three root causes: the so-called "three poisons" of addiction (greed or attachment), aversion, and delusion.[2]

THE THREE POISONS

Asian psychologies extend the scope of addiction beyond those objects such as drugs and food to which we usually limit it. Rather, they suggest that addiction can occur to practically any thing, person, or experience, including possessions, relationships, beliefs, and self-images.

Addiction is associated with the belief that "I must have (money, power, praise, or whatever) in order to be happy." It is a powerful dictator of feelings and fuels emotions such as jealousy, anger, and frustration. Because it says that I *must* have things a certain way, it reduces flexibility and choices. It also lies at the heart of such personality traits as miserliness and compulsive consumption.

Whereas addiction involves a compulsive need to experience and possess, aversion indicates a compulsive need to avoid. Fear, anger, defensiveness, and attack are its symptoms. For when there are things we feel we must avoid, we fear them, defend against them, become angry at the people or situations that create them, and feel justified in attacking and destroying them.

People and nations ruled by addiction and aversion are said to be slaves of every situation and environment, constantly preoccupied with a never ending quest to get what they want and avoid what they fear. For such people, happiness is limited to those occasions when the world is lined up to match their particular patterns of addiction and aversion. Thus, for example, a drug addict is at peace only when he gets his fix; the phobic only when the feared objects can be avoided or destroyed.

Unfortunately, there is a vicious cycle involved here. For successfully getting one's "fix" (be it drugs, possessions, or praise), or avoiding or attacking one's phobias (be they dirt, evil, communism, or capitalism), results in only temporary satisfaction. There is always something else to be desired or feared, and the process only further strengthens the addiction-aversion conditioning and its imprisoning stranglehold.[3]

When individual addictions or aversions are widespread they become reflected in the behavior of society. Thus, for example, addiction to material comforts results in lifestyles requiring ever increasing levels of consumption. These in turn require heavy energy and material imports and make us dependent upon foreign suppliers. We then become willing to go to war to defend "our vital interests" abroad. "The world has enough for everyone's need," said Gandhi, "but not enough for everyone's greed."

Eastern psychologies also point to how addicted we can become to beliefs and ideologies. We have already discussed the power of beliefs to shape perception and behavior. When to this is added the power of addiction, it is small wonder that whole cultures may live, kill, and die for their beliefs. The confrontation between the superpowers with their mutual threats of nuclear annihilation obviously represents a clash between addictions to different ideologies. To the force of these addictions is added that of aversion, which follows automatically and clearly lies at the root of a vast proportion of the world's hostility and aggression.

If, for example, we go beyond reasonable concern to extreme aversion of, say, either communism or capitalism, then our lives are dominated by obsessive preoccupation with, fear of, and hatred for them. We are continuously on the lookout for the first signs of their presence, fearful when we see them, fearful when we do not see them that we might have missed them, suspicious, even paranoid, of strangers lest they should turn out to be the dreaded enemy, willing to impoverish ourselves and others for defense, willing to indiscriminately embrace the most unsavory characters or countries provided only that they share our hatred. Witness, for example, Soviet support for a string of anti-American despots and American support for Pol Pot, the genocidal but anti-communist Cambodian responsible for the slaughter of two million of his countrymen.

In short, aversion manifests as both fear and hatred and lies at the root of an enormous amount of the world's suffering. The ancient Buddhists described it graphically and probably quite appropriately as spreading and consuming everything "like a forest fire" and recommended that it be thought of "like stale urine mixed with poison."[4]

The third of the three poisons, delusion, is also related to beliefs. Our usual state of mind, say Eastern psychologies, is neither clear, optimal, nor wholly rational. Rather, our addictions, aversions, and faulty beliefs color and distort our experience in important yet subtle, unrecognized ways. Because they are unrecognized, these distortions constitute a form of delusion (*maya* is what the Easterners call it), a form that is rarely appreciated because it is culturally shared.

Though such a claim may sound strange at first, it is actually consistent with the thinking of many eminent Western psychologists. "We are all hypnotized from infancy. We do not perceive ourselves and the world about us as they are but as we have been persuaded to see them," said Willis Harman of Stanford University.[5] "You see, very few of us are awake. I would say the majority of modern man lives in a verbal trance," claimed Fritz Perls,[6] the founder of Gestalt therapy. In recent years these claims have also found support from experimental studies.[7]

Both Eastern and Western psychologies agree, therefore, that our usual state of mind may be neither as clear nor as logical as we would like to believe. Perhaps the strongest statement of what this costs was made by the existentialist Ernest Becker, who said:

If we had to offer the briefest explanation of all the evil that men have wreaked upon themselves and upon their world since the beginning of time, it would be simply in *the toll that his pretense of sanity takes* as he tries to deny his true condition.[8]

Eastern psychologies would agree wholeheartedly.

These Eastern claims, then, are being echoed and studied increasingly by Western researchers.[9] Whatever their conclusions, it is hard to deny that there is much in the world and in our behavior that can only be regarded as insanity. "World is said to totter on 'brink of madness,'" cried the headline of a recent American Psychological Association publication reporting the conclusions of the World Congress on Mental Health.[10] The Eastern psychologies would agree and would suggest that the recognition of this insanity is essential for its cure and for the alleviation of the life-threatening global symptoms it has created. Perhaps it is only now, after they have brought us to the very edge of extinction, that we may be willing to recognize the full extent and destructiveness of our addictions, aversions, and delusions.

DUALISTIC THINKING AND PERCEPTION

Men are disturbed not by things, but by the view that they take of them.

Epictetus

Clearly, then, the three poisons of classical Buddhism provide valuable insights into our contemporary dilemma. But there is also another crucial factor mentioned by several Eastern psychologies. This factor is dualism: the fixation with seeing and thinking of everything primarily in terms of opposites— good and bad, black and white, in groups and out groups, us and them.

Not that dualism is necessarily bad. Of course we need dualism; we need to be able to recognize opposites. The problem is that we tend to become *fixated* on this particular way of seeing. But where we run into trouble is when we *only* recognize opposites and forget the commonality and unity that underlie them. Then we see not one planet, but only competing nations; not humankind, but only communists and capitalists, or men and women, or blacks and whites; not us, but me and them; not people with common human characteristics, but goodies and baddies.

How would you describe what is in the above frame? Well, there are two squares, left and right. Right! But now look at the frame below. What is in it? A rectangle, right? Right!

But that was also in the first frame! We just tended not to notice it because we focused on the dualism or dichotomy of the left and right squares. We tended to miss the whole or unity that underlies them and out of which they were carved.

Now notice something else about that first frame. You cannot have a left square without a right square and vice versa. You can only carve pairs of opposites out of unity. Try having a left side without a right side. You cannot magically create only one half of a dichotomy. The two halves depend on one another; they are interdependent. You cannot have lefts without rights, an "in" group without an "out" group. If you want to see some people as goodies, you have to see others as baddies; if I am determined to be the smart person in our relationship, you get to be—guess what—dumb. The smarter than you I need to seem, the dumber than me you have to appear. To the extent I see you primarily as dumb, to that extent I cannot recognize either our common humanity or that together we complement one another and make a complete couple. The Chinese Taoists were very aware of this and symbolized it with their famous yin-yang symbol.

Notice that the two halves are opposite and dependent on one another for their existence (remove one and the other disappears). They are also complementary (each provides what the other lacks, and the darker or bigger the one, the lighter or smaller appears the other). They are also complementary because they are parts of an underlying whole; together they create the perfect circle.

To summarize: Eastern disciplines suggest that a major cause of our problems, both individual and global, is our fixation on dualistic ways of seeing. This fixation means that we tend to lose sight of the wholeness, unity, and commonality that underlie all apparent opposites. In addition, we tend to forget that the opposites are created in part by our way of seeing and that they are complementary and dependent on one another for their existence.

But this is only the beginning of our troubles. Once we have perceived a duality, a pair of opposites, it is very hard for us not to end up valuing and becoming addicted to one half and devaluing and becoming averse to the other. One half is good, the other bad; one side right, the other necessarily wrong; half is pure, the other half evil, and so on. The more we like the one, the more we will dislike the other and vice versa.

To be addicted to having things one way is to develop aversion to other ways. It is also to lose sight both of the underlying commonality out of which the opposing halves were carved and of their interdependence. At this stage we are also likely to forget that whether we perceive opposition or complementarity it is, in part, our choice.

This fixation on dualistic seeing is the essence of conflict, and the perfect recipe for war.[11] For how could we wage battle unless we focused on the differences between us and our "enemy," on our good points and their bad, their malevolence and our altruism. And how could we attack unless, in focusing on our differences, we had overlooked our similarities and our shared humanity. Could a world such as our own, riddled by war and conflict, exist if on looking out at it, we saw not so much people different from and worse than us, but people like us? The Eastern psychologies say not. In the words of one of the early Zen masters uttered over a thousand years ago:

When love (addiction) and hate are both absent
everything becomes clear and undisguised.
Make the smallest distinction, however,
and heaven and earth are set infinitely apart. . . .
To set up what you like against what you dislike
is the disease of the mind. . . .
Be serene in the oneness of things
and such erroneous views will disappear by themselves.[12]

Modern science may not exactly be serene, but it is coming to recognize the oneness of things, and with that recognition some erroneous views are indeed disappearing. The old tendency to regard the world and ourselves as separate parts is giving way to a view of all things as interconnected and inter-dependent components of larger wholes. "The entire universe must, on a very accurate level, be regarded as a single indivisible unit," says modern physics.[13]

One approach to this kind of seeing is called "General Systems Theory," and it is a perspective that is having a major impact on contemporary think-ing. The anthropologist Gregory Bateson called it "the biggest bite out of the Tree of Knowledge in two thousand years."[14]

The general systems perspective echoes ancient wisdom: "We are not alone or separate"; "We are not apart from nature or our fellow humans"; "Everything we do affects everything else." To the extent we fail to recognize this interdependence and connectedness, to that extent we feel alienated, be-come ecologically insensitive, and are at risk for conflict with "others." Our current global crisis is making this fact desperately clear. "Confronting us with our mortality as a species it shows as the suicidal tendency inherent in our conception of ourselves as separate and competitive beings, and goads us to wake up to our interexistence."[15]

8

FEAR AND DEFENSE

Since wars begin in the minds of men, it is in the minds of men that we have to erect the ramparts of peace.

—*UNESCO Charter*

DEFENSE MECHANISMS

From the psychodynamic perspective, defense mechanisms constitute the heart of individual psychopathology. At both the individual and social levels, defense mechanisms offer rich insights into many aspects of our current dilemmas. One of the reasons for this becomes apparent if we remember that many of these dilemmas stem from our lack of awareness of their true nature, and that defense mechanisms operate by reducing and distorting awareness.[1] Moreover, defenses tend to create what they are designed to defend against. If we defend against a sense of insecurity and weakness, then the very defense tends to reinforce our belief in the reality of that weakness.

The defense mechanisms that appear particularly relevant to a discussion of global issues include repression, denial, projection, intellectualization, and rationalization.

"Humankind cannot bear very much reality," said T. S. Eliot, and repression and denial are the crutches we use to help us avoid it. One of the most persistent sources of despair to those working in these areas is the recognition of just how hard it is to sustain awareness of the true state of the world.[2] "I'd rather not think about it," "It's not really so bad," or, "It will all work out somehow," are just some of the statements that spring from repression and denial. Their result is "ostrichism," which narcotizes us and saps our motivation to respond in appropriate ways.

But the mechanisms of repression and denial extend further. We wish to deny not only the state of the world but also our role in producing it. Hence we use the mechanism of projection to attribute to others the unacknowledged aspects of our self-image and motives (what Jungians call the "shadow"), and thus create "the image of the enemy."[3]

This image is usually stereotypic and mirror-like. That is, no matter who "the enemy" is—Germans or British, Russians or Americans—they tend to be ascribed similar stereotypic traits and motives. These perceptions are mirrorlike because enemies tend to perceive each other similarly, each ascribing hostility and untrustworthiness to the other and seeing themselves as well-intentioned and benign. The process is further exacerbated by the "mote-beam phenomenon" that allows us to recognize the faults of others with crystal clarity while somehow missing our own. Moreover, what we deny in ourselves we tend to attack in others,[4] a process that clearly operates as destructively at the international level as it does at the interpersonal.

"The strain to consistency" then demands that this image of the enemy be maintained through selective perception and further defenses.[5] The "enemy's" behavior is now interpreted in ways consistent with the image. This leads us to attribute negative intentions to them and to view even hostility-reducing overtures as merely signs of deceit. Moreover, since we know how ethical and appropriate our own motives are, the fact that the enemy fails to acknowledge this, and even attributes their evil motivation to us, only further proves their duplicity.[6]

The result is a classical paranoid relationship. What was begun by the defense mechanisms of repression and projection is now exacerbated by self-fulfilling negative expectations and escalating suspicion, defensiveness, and hostility.

Once these distortions and paranoia are established they tend to elicit fearful defensive behavior that all too often is unethical and aggressive. Once this happens the disparity between our ethical righteous self-image and our not-so-ethical behavior demands explanation. Here is where the defense mechanism of rationalization charges to the rescue, firing off statements such as "We've got to do it," "There's no other way," or "It's for their own good." The most extreme examples of rationalization involve dehumanization, in which the enemy is seen as "not really human," or as an "animal."

All of this discussion is not to suggest that there is a shortage of sometimes aggressive and dishonest governments in the world. Rather, it is simply to point out that the situation is usually not nearly as black and white as most of us believe, and that international perceptions can be terribly distorted by a variety of psychological mechanisms that once set in motion, tend to assume a deadly inexorable momentum.[7]

Rationalization also occurs around other global problems. Faced with the uncomfortable recognition of the vast discrepancy between our own standard of living and that of the world's poor, we often feel obligated to justify the inequality and our failure to do more to relieve it. One form this takes is the so-called "fair world syndrome," in which we assume that the world is basically fair and that the suffering of the poor must therefore be their own fault. Common examples include, "It's their own fault for having too many children," "They could solve their problems themselves if they wanted to," or, "They're just too lazy to work."

Another common rationalization is that we ourselves are too poor to be able to help even though our "poverty" may represent awesome wealth by the standards of the truly poor. A classic example came in a letter I received from a Congressman stating, "We can't afford to initiate more welfare programs to feed the poor of the world; nor can we afford to reduce defense spending."

As psychoanalysts and Buddhists have both made clear, defenses operate to reduce our awareness of suffering, not only in ourselves but also in the world. When this suffering must be discussed, its emotional impact can be reduced by the mechanism of intellectualization. This is the process by which emotionally charged issues are thought of or discussed in abstract emotionless terms. War often provides particularly powerful examples and "the language of military science has always been devoid of reference to killing people or creating suffering."[8]

This defense mechanism has reached new heights of sophistication among nuclear strategists, whose "nuke speak" is "a strange and bloodless language by which the planners of nuclear war drain the reality from their actions."[9] Abstract discussion of reentry vehicles (missile warheads), "countervalue" (the destruction of cities), and "collateral damage" (killing civilians) facilitates planning for, what is in stark reality, strategic methods of producing more deaths and destruction than have occurred in all human conflicts.

The American "Doublespeak Awards" are given annually by the National Association of English Teachers to public figures who use phrases that are "grossly deceptive, evasive, euphemistic, confusing, or self-contradictory." A well-earned 1983 award went to the Air Force colonel who described the Titan II missile, which regularly carries a nine-megaton warhead, as a "potentially disruptive re-entry system."

It seems that the words of Confucius, spoken over 2,000 years ago, still hold true: "If names be not correct, language is not in accordance with the truth of things. If language be not in accordance with the truth of things, affairs cannot be carried on to success."[10]

The net result of all these defense mechanisms is "psychic numbing."[11] This is a narcotizing of our awareness that denies the world's reality (and our own), replacing it with distorted self-serving illusions that justify our misperceptions and deceptions, fuel our addictions and aversions, separate and alienate us from others, and further exacerbate the problems they were created to deny.

FEAR

When these defenses, distortions, addictions, and aversions are examined, we can see that they represent unskillful attempts to deal with fear. From this perspective, current international and nuclear threats can be seen as expressions of fear: fear of attack, fear for our survival, fear of losing our comforts, lifestyles, ideologies, and economic supplies.

What is crucial to recognize here is that a vicious cycle is operating: fear leads to misperceptions, defensiveness, weapons buildups, and aggressive posturing. These in turn lead to yet more fear, and this only further fuels defensiveness. The result is an escalating cycle of fear and defense, demanding ever more and more powerful responses. The billions of dollars spent on arms each day, the thousands of nuclear weapons, the millions of soldiers kept in readiness—all these are expressions of fear, expressions that create still more fear and demand still more defenses.

9

"WHERE ARE THE GROWN-UPS?" PSYCHOLOGICAL AND SOCIAL IMMATURITY

I have no doubt whatever that most people live, whether physically, intellectually or morally, in a very restricted circle of their potential being. They make use of a very small portion of their possible consciousness . . . much like a man who, out of his whole bodily organism, should get into a habit of using and moving only his little finger. . . . We all have reservoirs of life to draw upon, of which we do not dream.

—*William James*

Fear, greed, aversion, ignorance, unwillingness to delay gratification, defensiveness, and unconsciousness—these are marks of psychological immaturity. They point to the fact that global crises reflect more than the gross psychopathology of, say, a Hitler. They also reflect the myriad forms of "normal" psychological immaturity, inauthenticity, and failed actualization. This is perhaps most evident in politics, where decisions of enormous impact can be shaped by personal insecurities, personality foibles, and interpersonal jealousies.[1]

In ordinary daily life, such individual immaturity is usually regarded as unexceptional. "What we call 'normal' in psychology," said Abraham Maslow, the so-called father of humanistic psychology, "is really a psychopathology of the average, so undramatic and widely spread that we don't even recognize it ordinarily."[2] We do not recognize it because practically all of us share it in one form or another and because its impact is usually limited to our immediate contacts.*

With the awesome leverage of our technological and organizational power, the impact of these immaturities can become magnified into literally

---

*These widespread immaturities are no mere theoretical concepts. They have been demonstrated repeatedly by research which suggests that most of us are far from full psychological potential. For example, few people have attained fully mature levels of ego development.[6,7] Likewise only two percent of the population operates from the sixth (the second highest) level of Kohlberg's scale of moral development, and people who attain the highest level are very rare indeed.

41

earth-shattering proportions. Because of this magnification, the world now functions as a feedback system on which our immaturities and inauthenticities are "writ large" and reflected back to and onto us.

As at the individual, so also at the social level! Just as the fears, illusions, and defenses that create our global crises reflect individual immaturity, so too do they appear to reflect cultural immaturity and pathology. Our social goals, values, and norms appear to be partly created by, and reinforcing of, these individual fears, illusions, and defenses.

From this perspective, culture can be seen as more than just a force for education and evolution. It is also as a shared conspiracy against self-knowledge and psychological growth in which we collude together to protect one another's defenses and illusions. This sounds like an extreme statement, yet it is hardly a new one; psychologists have been echoing it for years. "The effect of society is not only to funnel fictions into our consciousness, but also to prevent awareness of reality," said Erich Fromm.[3] Others see culture as a shared hypnosis,[4] as a collaborative attempt to deny death,[5] or as a system facilitating substitute gratifications as much as authenticity and maturity.[6]

Other examples could be given, but the general point should be clear. The threats to our survival can be traced to psychological and social immaturities, inauthenticities, and pathologies. These are both created by and expressed through the symptoms of faulty beliefs, fear, defensiveness, and so forth, that we have already examined. In the future we will need to give more attention to the important role of social forces in creating and curing global problems. However, since effective responses begin with individuals, it is individual psychology that is emphasized in this book.

If immaturity is a cause of our difficulties then obviously survival may depend on our individual and collective maturation. Feedback is an essential aspect of learning, and the question naturally arises as to whether we can skillfully use the current global feedback to accelerate our maturation. This crucial question is discussed in detail in a subsequent section.

IN SUMMARY

In summary, then, the crises we face today, though unprecedented in scope, complexity, urgency, and potential for disaster, all have their roots in psychological causes and mechanisms. These causes—though themselves complex and exacerbated by political, social, and economic factors—stem fundamentally from our own psyches. The state of the world, in other words, reflects the state of our minds, and the causes of our current dilemmas must therefore be sought within us.

A psychological perspective therefore appears to offer valuable and unique insights into our contemporary condition. In addition, it may also complement and strengthen approaches that see global difficulties in terms of, for example, economic or political causes.

If the source of our difficulties is psychological, then it follows logically enough that any real cure must also include this psychological dimension. This is the fundamental assumption on which is based the following discussion, as well as the entire proposal for a psychology of human survival.

It is the mind which maketh good or ill
That maketh wretch or happy, rich or poor.

Edmund Spenser

• PART 3 •

TO HEAL A PLANET

10

GLOBAL THERAPY

From now on, it is only through a conscious choice and then deliberate policy that humanity can survive.

—*Pope John Paul II*

Can we apply our psychological understanding to contemporary crises and effectively become therapists to the world? At first such an idea may seem ridiculous, laughable in its hubris, naive in its belief that anyone, especially national leaders, would listen to us, and Pollyannaish in its optimism. Cynicism and despair may seem more realistic responses. Yet cynicism and despair are among the causes of our difficulties and must themselves be subject to psychological exploration if we are to move beyond immobilization to contribution.[1]

Yes, it is true that we cannot know whether we will succeed. It is also true that our best efforts may seem insignificant when measured against the vastness of ignorance, delusion, and suffering in the world. It is also true that it may seem easier to avoid the issues entirely and to succumb willingly to the "tranquilization by the trivial" so widely offered us by our culture. But it is also true that such tranquilization is purchased only at great cost to personal authenticity and well-being, and, if sufficient numbers opt for this decision, perhaps also at the cost of our planet and species.

Therefore, though to try to alleviate our global crises costs us a recognition of our limitations, not to try may cost us far more. "Almost anything you do will seem insignificant," said Gandhi, "but it is very important that you do it." Let us therefore confront our fears of hubris and hopelessness and see how we might apply our skills at the global level. For as Erich Fromm concluded in the last interview of his life, "We must not give up . . . we must try everything to avert disaster."[2]

Perhaps it will be helpful to consider a more familiar example: a family. Imagine, then, a family in which the parents have fallen into chronic conflict, paranoia, are threatening to kill one another, and are squandering their limited resources on weapons, while all around them their children and relatives suffer, sicken, starve, and die. All of us would regard this as an urgent situation, demanding immediate intervention. Indeed, anyone who failed to intervene would probably be regarded not only as without compassion, but also as unethical. Yet such is the condition of our human family today, and compassion, ethicality, and self-interest call upon us all to offer help in whatever ways we can. Of course, this is not to deny the enormously greater complexity of the global situation or the limits on extrapolating from families to nations.* However, we must start somewhere, and it makes sense to start by extrapolating from the simple to the complex. Let us therefore see if we can apply our psychological insights from this example to suggest skillful therapeutic responses to global crises.

The following, then, are hypothesized principles for effective responses. Each principle is presented as an hypothesis, since the situations we face are unprecedented and hypotheses are all that can truthfully be offered. At this stage, dogmatic beliefs are part of the problem rather than part of the solution.

---

*It is also not to imply that nations can be regarded simply as big people, or big families, or that all national and international behavior can be understood solely in terms of the psychology and behavior of individuals (reductionism). But it is to suggest that understanding the psychological factors that move individuals to behave in ways that create or correct global problems may be crucial to our survival.

11

BELIEFS AND EDUCATION

Do not put faith in traditions, even though they have been accepted for long generations and in many countries. Do not believe a thing because many repeat it. Do not accept a thing on the authority of one or another of the Sages of old, nor on the ground that a statement is found in the books. Never believe anything because probability is in its favor. Do not believe in that which you yourselves have imagined, thinking that a God has inspired it. Believe nothing merely on the authority of your teachers or of the priests. After examination, believe that which you have tested for yourselves and found reasonable, which is in conformity with your well-being and that of others.

—*The Buddha*

THE NECESSITY OF MULTIPLE RESPONSES

Where do you start?
We start everywhere at once.

Aldous Huxley

Often when we view the world from our particular vantage point we tend to focus on only one particular type of response. But since the problems and their causes are multiple, it follows that our responses should be also. At this time of crisis we need all the help we can get. It follows therefore that:

1. Skillful actions will tend to include different perspectives, approaches, and groups of people.
2. Optimal responses will include work on both symptoms *and* causes, including the psychological.
3. Skillful responses will modify our own psychology and behavior as well as that of others.

For example, it will be important for us *both* to feed the starving *and* address the political, economic, and psychological forces that allowed them to starve. It will be essential both to reduce nuclear stockpiles *and* study the factors contributing to international hostility.

THOUGHTS AND BELIEFS

The thought manifests as the word,
The word manifests as the deed,
The deed develops into habit,
And the habit hardens into character.
So watch the thought and its ways with care,
And let it spring from love
Born out of concern for all beings.

Anonymous

Since beliefs affect us so powerfully, it makes obvious sense for us to recognize and choose them skillfully. This process of recognizing and choosing beliefs is a widely used therapeutic technique employed by many different schools of psychology.[1] Each of them aims at replacing inaccurate, limiting, pathology-producing thoughts and beliefs with healthier ones.

Combinations of beliefs constitute images: of ourselves, of others, of the world, and of the future. Considerable evidence suggests that "the underlying images held by a culture or person have an enormous influence on the fate of the holder."[2] When traditional images lag behind cultural progress and do not adequately address novel situations and demands, then a period of social frustration, turmoil, and even crisis develops. Various indicators suggest that our culture may be nearing, if it is not already at, such a stage.[3]

On the other hand, when a culture's dominant images are attractive and anticipatory, providing uplifting yet realistic visions of what might be, then they tend to lead and direct social change.[4]

In choosing our beliefs we are therefore also choosing the images that will guide, create, and pull us, along with our culture, into the future. "The world partly becomes—comes to be—how it is imagined," said Gregory Bateson,[5] thereby echoing the words of the Buddha 2,500 years earlier, who said:

We are what we think.
All that we are arises with our thoughts.
With our thoughts we make the world.[6]

The importance of choosing our thoughts, images, and beliefs carefully and consciously is a theme that has been echoed through the ages by sages of all cultures.

The following, then, are beliefs that may be skillful for us to adopt. They can be divided into:

1. Beliefs about the nature of beliefs
2. Beliefs about ourselves

3. Beliefs about others
4. Beliefs about the world
5. Beliefs about warfare and nuclear weapons

Beliefs About Beliefs

a. Beliefs operate as powerful, yet usually unrecognized, self-fulfilling prophecies.

This hypothesis and the evidence supporting it have already been discussed. It represents a foundation that may motivate the conscious examination and selection of individual and cultural beliefs in line with the next hypothesis.

b. Our ideologies are belief systems.

Our ideologies are only beliefs, guesses, approximations, and models of the world and are not "the truth." When we remember this, then there is perhaps less risk of becoming addicted to them, and killing and dying for them. Likewise, there may be less risk of denying the possible value and validity of alternative views.

c. It is possible for us to choose skillful beliefs.

Sidestepping the never ending debate over free will versus determinism, this belief suggests that, like the great American philosopher William James, we can "will to believe." That is, we are free to choose consciously what we want to believe.[7] We do not have to be helpless victims of our beliefs, though the exquisite paradox is that we can choose to believe that we are.

In choosing our beliefs we move from being their passive victims to being their active creators. This enables us to recognize and help change limiting and distorting beliefs, not only in our own lives but also in society and the world. For example, "I can't," becomes "Perhaps I can"; "They are completely evil," might be changed to "Perhaps they are not all bad"; "You can't do anything with them," becomes "Perhaps if we tried a different approach," and so on.

At first, this process of questioning and changing beliefs may be uncomfortable, even fearful. For to question them requires a willingness to admit that we may have been mistaken, that things may not be as we thought they were, and that, at a fundamental level, we just do not know for sure how we or the world work.

Nor is this process of questioning and changing beliefs something that happens only once. Rather, it continues again and again for as long as we are willing to acknowledge our ignorance and to learn.*

---

*The process and its difficulties have been described exquisitely as follows:

Beliefs About Ourselves

Skillful beliefs about ourselves empower us and acknowledge our ability and desire to contribute to human survival. They serve as antidotes to the crippling effects of unworthiness and inadequacy created by beliefs such as, "There is nothing I can do," "No one would listen to me," "I can't," "I'm not qualified to . . . ." The following beliefs are designed to counter these self-imposed limits.

a. I (and each of us) can make a useful and unique contribution.
The importance of this belief is supported by considerable experimental evidence. Several studies show that our beliefs about our effectiveness function as self-fulfilling prophecies.[8] This principle was also stated decades ago by that great American psychologist Henry Ford, who said, "Those who believe they can do something and those who believe they can't are both right."[9]

b. Contributing to human survival may be something we deeply desire and find deeply satisfying.
This belief helps us recognize that contributing need not be experienced as a sacrifice, but rather may be genuinely and deeply desired. The desire to contribute appears to be deeply rooted in all of us [10] but is often hidden under feelings of unworthiness and inadequacy.

c. Developing and applying a psychology of human survival may be a particularly strategic contribution that we can make.
This belief is, of course, the reason for this book. It suggests that whatever our particular contributions may be, they may be more effective if done in accordance with sound psychological principles.

Beliefs About Others and Our Relationship to Them

Skillful choices here would counter beliefs that tend to degrade, dehumanize, blame, and attack others or separate and alienate us from them. Beliefs that

---

"This is why it is so difficult to explain the path to one who has not tried: he will see only his point of view of today or rather the loss of his point of view. And yet if we only knew how each loss of one's viewpoint is a progress and how life changes when one passes from the stage of the closed truth to the stage of the open truth—a truth like life itself, too great to be trapped by points of view, because it embraces every point of view . . . a truth great enough to deny itself and pass endlessly into a higher truth."[16]

This process of continuously relinquishing the old and creating anew, of letting go yesterday's truths and allowing tomorrow's to emerge, of repetitively giving up what was in order to find what might be, of continuous death and rebirth, is the very essence and essential of growth in both individuals,[17] and cultures.[18] For to cling fearfully to the old and familiar, the "good old days" and ways (archaism), rather than allowing them to pass when their time has come, is to attempt to freeze the universal process of continuous death and rebirth (palingenesis) out of which our potentials emerge.

52

heighten empathy and trust and acknowledge our shared humanity may be helpful, as for example:

a. Despite different cultural and ideological backgrounds, we all share a common humanity with similar joys, sufferings, hopes, and fears.

b. Greater familiarity with others will develop greater empathy and understanding.
This is why so many people—psychologists, political scientists, and religious leaders—have emphasized the importance of direct personal contact between leaders and peoples from nations in conflict.

c. Our expectations (beliefs) of others tend to be self-fulfilling.
This old idea has found recent experimental support. It follows, therefore, that:

d. It is skillful to trust rather than to distrust.
Experiments suggest that giving others the benefit of the doubt may be a skillful way of eliciting trustworthy behavior. In order to understand this, we need to make a distinction between willingness to trust and gullibility. Contrary to popular belief, they are not the same, and recent studies suggest that high trusters are no more likely to be victimized than low trusters. They are, however, likely to be happier, more likeable, and psychologically healthy, and more trustworthy themselves.[11]

Beliefs About the World

Every thought you have makes up some segment of the world you see.
It is with your thoughts, then, that we must work,
if your perception of the world is to be changed.

Anonymous

a. The global threats to human survival and well-being can be solved.
Here lies one of the fundamental beliefs about the world on which rests our fate. In its broad scope it encompasses beliefs about individual problems such as: we can grow enough food, alleviate poverty, limit nuclear weapons, reduce pollution, and stabilize the ecosystem. Without beliefs such as these, we are left with hopelessness and despair and with no motivation even to begin the healing work that is so desperately needed.

b. These problems are among the most urgent and important priorities confronting us all.
This may sound like an obvious, even trite, statement. But how many of us really live our lives as though it were true? Don't most of us pay more

attention to our golf scores, our paychecks, and our sex lives, than to the fact that life itself is threatened? Do our daily lives reflect our true priorities and those of our planet? To the extent that we acknowledge the importance of global issues, to that extent will our personal priorities reflect the truth of our situation rather than a denial of it. As we will discuss in a later chapter, this re-ordering of our personal priorities may prove to be not a sacrifice, but rather a deep enrichment of the quality of our own lives.

Beliefs About Warfare and Nuclear Weapons

It seems particularly important to question current ideas about nuclear weapons that, if incorrect, would result in incomprehensible disaster or even planetary suicide. Beliefs that perform this questioning include:

a. Nuclear superiority may be unattainable.

b. Once begun, it may be impossible to limit the size of a nuclear war.

c. Nuclear war may be unwinnable.

d. Large-scale nuclear war may result in such destruction and ecological disruption as to destroy civilization in any meaningful form.

These beliefs obviously call into question the nuclear strategies of both the Soviet Union and the United States.

There are two beliefs that may be crucial to reversing the ever-increasing arms buildup. The first is that:

e. It may be possible to reduce and even eliminate nuclear weapons.

It is often argued that it is Pollyannaish to believe that we can eliminate, or even significantly reduce, nuclear weapons. They cannot be uninvented, goes the argument, and to reduce them would mean unsettling the balance of power. A world without nuclear weapons is "a fictional utopia," states a group of Harvard professors, who conclude that, "Living with nuclear weapons is our only hope." [12]

The danger of such arguments (beliefs) should be apparent. If we believe that nuclear stockpiles cannot be safely reduced or eliminated then we have no motivation to make any serious attempt to do so. Yet, as should have become painfully apparent by now, our current situation—with billions of tons of TNT explosive power, with hairpin trigger warning systems, with unstored toxic waste products, and with accidents of some sort occurring almost daily—is so fraught with danger as to almost eclipse the dangers of disarmament. "The risks inherent in disarmament pale in comparison to the risks inherent in an unlimited arms race," said President Kennedy to the United Nations, which itself unanimously passed a resolution that stated: "The question of complete disarmament is the most important one facing the world today." [13] If this is the most important question facing the world then it seems important to start by choosing to believe that we *can* answer it.

Similar issues underlie the closely related belief that:

f. It may be possible to reduce or eliminate the arms trade.

"The idea that this can be eliminated is ridiculous"; "So many people, industries, and nations are dependent on it that there would be widespread economic collapse"; "People would never agree to abolishing it." Do these arguments sound familiar? They should! They were staunchly believed and vehemently fought for only a century ago in response to talk of abolishing slavery. Today slavery is not only abolished, but almost universally abhorred. Yet today the arms trade kills more people every few years than the slave trade did over centuries. One reason for this is that we believe the arms trade is acceptable, even essential, exactly as our forefathers believed about the slave trade.

g. War can no longer be regarded as a legitimate means of obtaining national goals.

For as long as we regard wars as legitimate and appropriate for getting what we want, for that long will we be at risk of dying in them. Yet the more destructive our weapons and wars, the more obviously questionable become their legitimacy and appropriateness.

Of course, none of this is to suggest that reducing or eliminating wars, nuclear weapons or the arms trade will be a simple task. It is not even to suggest that we will necessarily succeed. But it is to suggest that it is terribly, terribly important for us to be wary of beliefs that the task is impossible.

These, then, are some of the beliefs that may provide a basis for (a psychology of) human survival. Together they may encourage self-fulfilling realism and optimism toward the world, responsibility and effectiveness in ourselves, and empathy and understanding for others.

When beliefs are examined closely, it becomes apparent that all statements (including this one) contain them. In fact, all our assumptions and statements about ourselves, others, and the world are based on them. When this is recognized, the profound importance of becoming more aware of our beliefs and choosing them carefully and consciously becomes, I believe, strikingly apparent. We sorely need to be educated about our beliefs, which brings us to our next topic.

EDUCATION

Human history becomes more and more a race between education and
catastrophe.

H. G. Wells

As we discussed earlier, many destructive beliefs and behaviors can be
traced to simple ignorance of our situation. It therefore follows that:

1. Corrective education is essential.

Obviously we need widespread information about the state of the world.
We also need accurate, unbiased information about conflicting ideologies and
people. As we have discussed, groups in conflict tend to adopt rigid, stereo-
typed images of one another, and this process is exacerbated when adequate
information is lacking. Unfortunately, the withholding of information is all
too often adopted as deliberate policy. In Iron Curtain countries, information
about the West is heavily censored, while in the United States there existed
for many years "the unwritten law that Americans remain entirely ignorant of
Soviet communism. Teachers were fired for teaching about it; people lost
jobs for reading about it." [14] Unfortunately, we tend to be particularly fearful
of the unknown. The net result of this ignorance is therefore that billions of
dollars are spent out of fear of people who exist in one another's minds partly
as shadow figures constructed from misinformation and myth.

However, ignorance is not the only reason for destructive beliefs and behavior. The whole menagerie of psychological defenses and distortions that
we examined earlier also plays its part, and therefore,

2. To be most effective, education should include information about both
the state of the world around us and the psychological forces within us that
create it. And of course,

3. Education should be of both ourselves and others.

As always, the ignorance of others is obvious; our own less so. This education should of course include children, for as Jerome Frank points out: "For
the long pull, main reliance must be placed on the education and training of
upcoming generations." [15]

The importance of education becomes even more apparent if we accept
the idea that:

4. Knowing the facts tends to evoke appropriate responses.

It was for reasons such as these that sages and educators from Socrates on
have extolled the importance of education as crucial for social well-being. In
our own time, it has also become crucial for global well-being and survival,
for as Albert Einstein said, "Peace cannot be kept by force. It can only be
achieved by understanding."

12

SUGGESTIONS FROM BEHAVIOR MODIFICATION: REINFORCERS AND THE MEDIA

Whatever you can do, or dream you can—begin it.
Boldness has genius, power, and magic in it.

—*Goethe*

REINFORCERS

Many ecological and international stresses can be traced to unfortunate reinforcement patterns built into our social and economic systems. It follows that a global psychology will want to identify these and point to alternate patterns that reward ecologically and internationally sensitive choices.

In identifying these factors we would want to take into account the following ideas:

1. It will be important to provide greater reinforcement for decisions that take long-term effects into account.

For example, at the present time politicians receive very little reinforcement for decisions that limit the use of nonrenewable resources such as oil. Rather, the reverse is true. Consumers want, and hence reinforce politicians for, decisions that provide unlimited supplies *now*. Tomorrow is left to take care of itself. This provides a powerful example of the link between the addictions and reinforcers motivating the public and those motivating economic and political decision makers. If we want to radically change politicians' decisions we will also have to radically change what we want.

2. Increased information and feedback on the costs and benefits, particularly long-term ones, of economic, industrial, and legislative decisions may be important.

So often the subtle, long-term ecological effects of our decisions are ignored at first, only to exact a growing toll with the passage of time. Environmental impact reports provide a valuable example of possible approaches to this problem. They make both long-term and geographically distant effects harder to ignore and provide reinforcement for decisions that take them into account.

57

3. Where possible, decision makers should directly experience, and not be unduly or unequally shielded from, the effects of their decisions.

In many countries, legislators exempt themselves from the laws they pass, such as mandatory retirement and military service, or are shielded from experiencing the effects of their decisions. For example, a war may cost the lives of thousands upon thousands of people, yet the leader who started it may never see a single drop of blood. How much harder it might be to start wars if this were not so. Roger Smith, a Harvard lawyer, wryly suggested an antidote, as follows:

Whenever the President of the United States goes anywhere he is followed at a discreet distance by a military officer carrying a small briefcase. Inside that briefcase is the combination to the end of civilization: the codes by which the President can order a nuclear attack. It is a simple matter: take the key, open the briefcase, transmit the codes, head for shelter, and the war (and civilization) is as good as over. A similar system probably operates in the Soviet Union.

Roger Smith's suggestion is elegantly and bizarrely simple. Instead of carrying the codes in the case, implant them in a capsule near the military aide's heart. Place in the briefcase a knife. Now in order to get the code and give the orders killing a billion or more people, the President must first kill the aide himself.

Of course the suggestion is not serious, but the point it makes is. It may be easier to give orders meaning the death of multitudes than it may be to kill a single person oneself. Roger Smith may be a lawyer but he is also a shrewd psychologist, intuitively aware of the dangers of social and military systems that shield leaders from directly experiencing the effects of their choices. It may be impossible to compel national leaders to ride at the head of their armies as in days of yore. However, it may be possible and advisable, at least in democracies, to ensure that decision makers are not unduly shielded from the effects of their decisions.

4. Reinforcement patterns should be modified so as to reward ecologically sensitive lifestyles and consumption patterns.

Modern economic systems make no distinction between renewable and nonrenewable resources, only between cheap and expensive ones.[1] Therefore neither industrialists nor consumers are reinforced for ecologically sensitive choices. However, these choices could be reinforced by, for example, modifying taxes to raise the price of nonrenewable resources and reduce the cost of renewable ones.

As an example, let us look at energy supplies in the United States. The current system is sadly biased toward nonrenewable sources. Oil, coal, and natural gas receive billions of dollars of government subsidies each year, whereas renewable resources such as solar and wind get pennies by comparison.[2] Massive support for highways and low gasoline prices reinforce people for using cars. Fewer people then use public transportation, which has to raise prices, forcing still more people into their cars. The result is a vicious cycle of costly, shrinking public transportation and increasing numbers of American cars that now guzzle 6 percent of the world's energy. This cycle has occasionally received additional help from automobile manufacturers: in the 1920s General Motors purchased the Los Angeles rapid-transit rail system and then tore it up.[3]

Clearly many of our current economic reinforcement patterns are ecological disasters. If we want people to make ecologically sensitive choices we are going to have to reward them with ecologically sensitive reinforcers.

5. Voluntary simplicity may be just as satisfying (reinforcing) as high consumption.

> Consumption has been viewed as a primary end of human activity. This view is reflected in the customary measure of man's happiness—his "standard of living"—which is calculated almost exclusively in material terms. We have attempted to maximize consumption, implicitly assuming that the level of consumption is directly related to the level of human well-being and happiness. This seems an ill-founded and excessively limiting assumption for approaching the totality of human satisfaction.
>
> *Duane Elgin*[4]

If consumption and material comforts have been our goal then we in the West have succeeded beyond the wildest dreams of earlier generations. An average worker possesses resources and amusements undreamed of by Croesus or any ancient plutocrat. For most of us in the West the age-old dream of material comfort has been realized.

But are we truly happy? Happier perhaps, but hardly truly satisfied! Suffering and discontent remain widespread. People may worry less about food and shelter but worry more about a vague sense of meaninglessness, frustration, and disappointment.[5] The age-old dream has been realized, but its rewards have turned out to be partly illusory.

We are in a unique situation. For the first time in human history, the majority of a population has the chance to find out from personal experience that no amount of material possessions and comforts is sufficient to ensure happiness. Never before have so many of us been able to test for ourselves the age-old warning that purely material pursuits are ultimately unsatisfying.

It is a situation we could have predicted from what we know about desires and addictions. Remember that even when we get something we are addicted to—be it a drug, car, money, or sex—we are at risk for trouble. The satisfaction turns out to be only temporary, and soon we need not only another, but a bigger, better "fix" to get the same kick. This is the vicious cycle of increasing compulsive consumption and decreasing satisfaction. We can never get enough of what we do not really want, and as George Bernard Shaw pointed out, "There are two ways of being disappointed in life. One is not to get what you want and the other is to get it."

The result is a mounting sense of frustration, bewilderment, and dismay. The dream has been realized, yet not only do frustrations and dissatisfactions remain, but also questions of meaning and purpose loom even larger. Wordsworth described the problem poetically, saying:

The world is too much with us; late and soon.
Getting and spending, we lay waste our powers;
Little we see in nature that is ours;
We have given our hearts away.

Most people in this dilemma do not know where to turn for relief. The neverending message pouring forth from every medium is to increasingly "produce and consume the unnecessary."[6] It is hard to realize that deeper satisfaction may lie in doing exactly the opposite, and there is little encouragement for a life of greater simplicity.

But though there may be little encouragement, growing numbers of people are moving in this direction and seeing in voluntary simplicity a more mature, satisfying, enriching, and ecologically sensitive way of life. It must be emphasized that voluntary simplicity is not deprivation or sacrifice; it does not necessarily mean living alone in an unheated cabin. Rather, it is "an avoidance of external clutter, of many possessions irrelevant to the chief purpose of life. It means an ordering and guiding of our energy and our desires, a partial restraint in some directions in order to secure greater abundance of life in other directions."[7]

Duane Elgin, one of today's most thoughtful social scientists, summarizes it this way. Voluntary simplicity is a lifestyle that emphasizes conscious choiceful consumption in recognition of the fact that "voluntarily simplifying the external/material aspects of one's life may significantly contribute to the enrichment of internal/nonmaterial aspects."[8]

Of course this is hardly a new idea. It has been one of the central claims of the great religious sages and of more recent social activists such as Gandhi. "The fewer the necessities the greater the happiness," is the theme they echo.[9] "If you want to make a man happy add not to his riches but take away from his desires," warned the Greek philosopher Epicurus. From the wisdom of all cultures and ages comes the same message: that voluntary simplicity may be both a means to, and an expression of, psychological maturity and satisfaction.

And not just of individuals only. In his sweeping survey of human development, the great historian Arnold Toynbee found that mature cultures display "progressive simplification": an increasing focus on the more subtle nonmaterial satisfactions of life.

In our time the attraction of a simpler, less compulsive way of life may be coupled with the hard push of necessity.[10] We cannot long continue to consume as profligately and unthinkingly as we have. Our dwindling resources simply will not allow it. However, if we can extract ourselves from the hypnotizing, desire fueling messages bombarding us from the media, we may find that lifestyles of voluntary simplicity are not only economically, ecologically, and ethically appropriate, but also deeply satisfying and maturing.

To have but few desires and satisfaction with simple things is a sign of a superior man.[11]

6. International tensions might be reduced by choosing patterns of mutual reinforcement.

One of the characteristic features of unsuccessful marriages is that spouses give one another very little reinforcement. Affection goes unnoticed, help goes unappreciated, and attempts at reconciliation are misinterpreted. In other words, partners give each other very little reward for friendly, helpful behavior. Not surprisingly, they end up feeling unappreciated and less and less inclined to be friendly or to give reinforcement themselves. The result is a vicious cycle in which ever decreasing amounts of mutual reinforcement become both the result and the cause of further deterioration in the relationship.

On top of this, the spouses are likely to begin punishing one another. As fewer rewards are received, frustration and anger develop. The inevitable result is attack, and to the vicious cycle of diminishing reinforcement is now added an equally vicious cycle of mutual attack and punishment. It is a terribly familiar story, played out today and every day in literally hundreds of millions of homes across the world.

Recently, behaviorists have had significant success with marital therapy by teaching spouses about these principles of reinforcement.[12] The first steps are to help the partners become aware of the patterns they have trapped themselves in and to teach them the golden rule of behavior modification: "Reward people for what you want them to do." Do not just punish them for what they do wrong, reward them for what they do right.

Once partners know these principles then they can reverse the vicious cycle by reinforcing the friendly helpful gestures that they previously ignored. What this requires is that at least one partner is willing to make the first move toward reconciliation, to begin to relinquish vengeance and attack, and to start rewarding the other.

It seems likely that these principles can be extended to the international level. For example, it is painfully obvious that the cold war between the Western and Iron Curtain countries reflects half a century of minimal mutual reinforcement and high mutual punishment. These patterns both stem from and exacerbate other factors such as distrust, paranoia, and projection. The laws of reinforcement are no respectors of size, and nations that use them unskillfully fall victim to them just as marriage partners do. Unfortunately, however, the consequences are vastly different. What ends up as harsh words and threats of separation in one case, ends up as harsh words and threats of nuclear annihilation in the other.

On the positive side, it seems reasonable to think that application of behavioral principles might be helpful to international relations. Of course, skillful politicians probably recognize these principles intuitively, but increased awareness and conscious application of them might be lifesaving.

SOCIAL LEARNING THEORY AND THE MEDIA

Given the recent evidence of the awesome power of the media, their role in addressing global threats may be crucial.[13] Given also the evidence of just how unhelpful, even damaging, so much of the content of the current media is, it is obvious that our fate may depend on whether far-reaching changes are made.

At the present time the typical media diet of "tranquilization by the trivial" is offered with the rationale that, "that is what the public wants," even though evidence suggests otherwise.[14] Significant changes are therefore likely to occur only when enough people are willing to make their wants clear. We cannot realistically expect the media to change their traditional ways unless we change ours first. We can certainly apply the principle of reinforcing people for what we want them to do. Clearly, we need to reinforce media executives, politicians, and advertisers for globally sensitive choices and give them feedback (not anger and attack) for unskillful ones.

As always, the first thing we have to change to produce social and global changes is ourselves. Mental health professionals have much to contribute here. Their research has already demonstrated many harmful effects of current programming. These contributions can be expanded by further research and by ensuring that their findings are used to educate the public and legislators about the broader psychological, social, and global implications of media programming.

13

REDUCING FEAR AND
DEFENSIVENESS

Defense is frightening. It stems from fear,
increasing fear as each defense is made.
You think it offers safety.
Yet it speaks of fear made real and terror justified.

—Anonymous

If two of the major psychological forces jeopardizing our survival are fear and defensiveness, then one of our major tasks is to find ways of reducing them. The question is basically this: what can we do to develop a greater sense of mutual trust and safety? This is a familiar problem for family therapists, and their work suggests several useful principles. Perhaps the most important of these are:

1. To reduce threats and condemnation
2. To encourage honest, ethical behavior

REDUCING THREATS AND CONDEMNATION

The participants in the cold war are enmeshed in a vicious self-perpetuating cycle of mutual paranoia. Attack and counterattack follow one another in an endless cycle as each seeks an illusionary sense of security and righteousness through condemning and threatening the other.

Family therapists would suggest that the first task is to assist participants to appreciate the destructive, reciprocal, and self-perpetuating nature of this process. It must be recognized that condemnation and threats, though perhaps personally gratifying, are *not* particularly effective means of persuading opponents to do as you wish. Rather, they usually have the opposite effect by increasing fear, defensiveness, resistance, and resentment.

Only by reducing one's threats and condemnations is an antagonist's paranoia likely to be reduced. Less paranoia means less defensiveness and aggression, which in turn will enhance one's own sense of trust and safety.[1] Particularly when combined with greater mutually positive reinforcement, this approach might reverse the previous vicious cycle that has poisoned East-West relations for almost half a century.

ETHICALITY

Ours is a world of nuclear giants and ethical infants.

General Omar Bradley

At this moment some 3,000 intercontinental missiles sit in silos around the world, poised for launch at a moment's notice. In the air overhead bombers circle constantly lest they be caught on the ground by a surprise attack. And in the depths of the ocean, hidden from prying eyes and radar, glide the nuclear submarines. All of these forces are kept in constant readiness for a simple but tragic reason; the enemy is believed to be dishonest and unethical and quite capable of launching a surprise attack without provocation or warning. From this perspective the arms race can be seen as a result of a mutual belief that our adversaries are unethical and untrustworthy, as sometimes they certainly are.

If our adversaries' dishonesty and unethicality threaten our survival, then obviously it is appropriate to take countermeasures. Unfortunately, what all too often happens is that these countermeasures themselves include unethical methods. Of course these are regarded as regrettable but also as essential. A vicious cycle of escalating dishonest, unethical behavior grows out of fear and defensiveness and increases every step of the way. The tragic result is that "enemies become what they imagine each other to be."[2] How to reverse this cycle is one of the central questions of our time.

For family therapists this is a familiar problem. For them, almost every day brings another lesson in the costs of unethical behavior and the vicious cycles to which it leads. The therapeutic principles for treating families enmeshed in these cycles are well understood, and perhaps we can learn from them some principles applicable to the treatment of nations.

The first step is probably education. It is important first to become aware of the vicious cycle to which unethicality gives birth. Next, it is crucial to observe the heavy costs of this cycle, both to ourselves and others. For it is seeing the nature of the vicious cycle and the extent of its costs that provides the motivation to halt it and to begin acting more ethically.

However, greater honesty and ethicality by either side is initially likely to be regarded with suspicion by the other: "Is it a trick?" "Is it merely an attempt to get us off our guard?" they wonder. Only if one side persists in greater levels of honesty and ethicality can the other eventually begin to feel less threatened, less defensive, and more trusting. With less fear and defensiveness it is now possible that they too may in turn become more honest and ethical themselves. With this, the cycle may be broken and reversed.

These are familiar therapeutic principles. But there are further advantages to ethicality, advantages that are less well known because they come to us from the Eastern psychologies.

These psychologies point out that unethical behavior is motivated by more than fear and defensiveness. Further destructive forces include addiction and aversion, as well as others such as jealousy and laziness. Moreover, although all behavior originates from the mind, it also leaves its imprint on the mind and tends to reinforce the factors that elicited it. Therefore, unethical behavior tends to reinforce the emotions such as greed, anger, and jealousy that evoke it. The end result is yet another vicious cycle in which the mind is left still more deeply enmeshed in painful destructive conditioning.[3]

The way to break this intrapsychic cycle is also by a commitment to greater ethicality. For to experience emotions such as fear or greed, which motivate unethical behavior, yet not to act on them, is to diminish and conquer them. It is also to cultivate their opposites, such as courage, generosity, and calm, as well as a more positive self-image.[4] The net effect is that ethicality enhances psychological growth and maturity. That is why it is a central component of every major Eastern growth discipline.

There is one other approach that Eastern psychologies suggest for reducing animosity, fear, and defensiveness, and it is exquisite in its simplicity. It is this: give to your "enemy" a gift.[5] It is hard to feel angry and defensive when receiving a gift, but it is also hard to feel that way when giving one. What a different world this might be if we gave gifts not only to those we already appreciate, but also to those we need to learn to appreciate.

14

REINTERPRETING MOTIVATION

*You respond to what you perceive,
and as you perceive so shall you behave.*

—Anonymous

The way in which we respond to people depends not only on what they do to us but also on what we believe they want to do to us. How we interpret and perceive their motives therefore determines our responses. If we think someone is criticizing us out of hatred and malevolence we will probably reciprocate. But if we perceive the same behavior coming from fear and insecurity we are more likely to understand and forgive. For us as for Shakespeare, "There is nothing good or bad but thinking makes it so."

This becomes all the more crucial in light of Abraham Maslow's study of motivation. Maslow[1] distinguished between motives based primarily on inadequacy, need, or deficiency and those stemming from sufficiency or well-being. Every motive, he thought, fell into one of these two categories. Every act either attempted to compensate for deficiency or expressed well-being.

It follows that everything we say or do—and everything anyone else says or does to us—is either an expression of sufficiency and well-being or one of deficiency and fear. To see this is to gain a very different and very important perspective on everyone's behavior, including our own. The critical question is whether we are able to recognize the underlying deficiency and fear, even when they are expressed as, for example, anger, jealousy, and attack. If we can recognize them, we will likely respond in ways that heal. If not, we will likely attack and only further exacerbate them.

This ability to recognize underlying fear and deficiency is a basis for both successful psychotherapy and for the development of compassion and forgiveness. For to see another person's motives truly is to feel with and understand them. From understanding comes an automatic relinquishment of anger and resentment, for as the French proverb has it, "To understand all is to forgive all." That is why the deepest form of forgiveness is not a forceful suppression of righteous anger but an automatic relinquishment in the light of understanding.

From forgiveness comes healing. For the fear, insecurity, and defensiveness from which came the original attack have not been further exacerbated by being themselves attacked. Rather, they have been understood, and in the face of nonjudgmental understanding they are unnecessary.

Forgiveness, however, benefits not just the receiver but also the person who gives it. When we fail to recognize fear and deficiency we see instead evil and malevolence. Then we judge and condemn, become angry and attack. Those we do not forgive we fear and attack, and although we often forget it, we are the victims of our fear and anger as much as the people we attack. After all, the emotions we direct at others exist first in our own minds. For this same reason, if we understand and forgive others then we too share the benefits.

That is why the deeper levels of forgiveness are mutually beneficial. It is also why the deeper teachings of all the great religions see it as a powerful growth tool and do not advocate condemning, crushing, or destroying evil, but of understanding and forgiving it. For "A mind beyond judgments watches and understands,"[2] and people of such a mind, said Lao Tzu, the founder of Taoism, "only pursue an offender to show him the way."[3]

Note that compassion and forgiveness do not imply passivity or denial. They do *not* mean allowing someone to walk all over you or take advantage of you. Nor do they imply a Pollyannaish denial of the existence of destructive motives such as greed and self-aggrandizement. Rather, they represent a denial of the denial of the underlying fear and deficiency that power them.

The implications of these ideas are both powerful and challenging. For it follows that if we would be effective agents for change and human survival our task is not to attack those we see as endangering us and our planet, but rather to understand and forgive them. This is no small challenge. It is much easier and initially more satisfying to judge and attack than it is to empathize with those we fear or hate.

Yet it is fear and hate that have created so many of our current problems. The cold war and the arms race are undeniable examples. Is it realistic to think that adding still more fear and hate to the genocidal levels already existing will really be helpful? Or will we just be venting our own personal frustrations, and purchasing a sense of righteous superiority at everyone else's cost?

These principles therefore seem to apply at the international level as well as the interpersonal. If we can be more aware of the fear, insecurity, and deficiency that underlie so many international tensions, then perhaps we can begin to cut through automatic responses such as fear and paranoia, and then condemnation, anger, and attack.[4] This would help short-circuit the vicious cycles of paranoia and recrimination. A deeper understanding of motivation may therefore provide a strategic means for breaking out of the morass of endless accusations and counteraccusations that characterizes so many international relations and threatens to end all relations.

15

RECOGNIZING THE SELF
WE SHARE

See yourself in others.
Then whom can you hurt?
What harm can you do?

—*The Buddha*

Therapists who work with disturbed families or organizations are well aware that one of their first and most important tasks is to help their clients recognize areas of shared purpose and experience. As global psychologists for our disturbed planet we would want to do the same.

Such an approach is now all the more important because so many of our contemporary difficulties are no respectors of traditional boundaries. Our various economic, social, and cultural systems are becoming increasingly interdependent. The threat that some impoverished countries might be unable to repay the tens of billions of dollars of loans they have received sends shock waves through the international financial community. A recession in the United States leaves millions unemployed throughout the world. Ecological imbalances, atmospheric pollution, and radioactive contamination do not halt politely at international borders. With each new disruption it becomes more apparent that our biosphere—the totality of earth, water, air, plants, and animals—functions as an interconnected whole. A change in any part affects every part. Increasingly, we are forced to recognize that what we do unto others we are also doing unto ourselves. As Jerome Frank put it, "The psychological problem is how to make all people aware that whether they like it or not, the earth is becoming a single community."[1]

As global therapists we would therefore want to help each other recognize that so many of the problems we face are shared; that they threaten each and every one of us. We would want to recognize, for example, the widespread economic, social, and psychological costs of the arms race. We would also want to be aware of the ways in which poverty heightens national and international tensions, restricts trade, imposes suffering on the poor, and demands unconsciousness and defensiveness in the wealthy.

The fact that these threats and costs are common to us all is a particularly important and, funnily enough, hopeful sign. Hopeful because shared threats are powerful forces for encouraging collaboration and friendship. When people face a common threat they share a common purpose, and when they share a common purpose they tend to forget past differences and unite for their common good. This is particularly true when the challenge is greater than any one group can handle alone, and experiments show that cooperation on such tasks may be the most effective way of resolving mutual hostility.[2] For all these reasons and more it will be vital for our survival to encourage cooperation. In our increasingly interdependent world it may well be that, as Martin Luther King, Jr. said, "We will live together as brothers or die together as fools."

We would also want to acknowledge our shared humanity underlying the cultural and ideological differences that appear to separate and make us strangers or even enemies to each other. Certainly we would want to acknowledge that we all share to some degree the fears, misunderstandings, and defenses that have created our conflicts and difficulties. But we would also want to acknowledge our common human strengths; the shared hopes, ideals, and altruism that make us seek for the happiness and well-being, love and belongingness, that we all desire.

Our task, then, is to work to shift our perception from a focus on our differences to a focus on our similarities, from a dualistic emphasis on conflicting groups and cultures to a unitive appreciation of our shared humanity, from a fragmentary view that sees us apart from nature, and nature itself in parts, to a holistic vision that recognizes the unity and interconnection of all parts. Each person we meet, every situation, every interaction presents us with a choice. We choose whether to set ourselves apart from others or whether to look past the otherness to the self we share; whether to see ourselves as separate and independent from others and the world or affecting and affected by all.

It is not a minor choice. For in the way we choose to see ourselves and our relationship to the world may hang its fate and ours. The central human problem, said the great humanistic psychiatrist Erich Fromm,[3] is "How to overcome separateness, how to achieve union, how to transcend one's individual life and find at onement." For "wherever there is other there is fear."[4]

Fortunately, a shift in the right direction appears to have begun. The editor of the journal *Foreign Affairs* wrote:

Something beyond nationalism is slowly taking root in the world . . . the signs of a developing sense of common human destiny are present . . . world affairs will have a very dim future if this international sentiment fails to show a steady increase from now on.[5]

Albert Einstein agreed and went further, saying:

A human being is a part of the whole called by us universe, a part limited in time and space. He experiences himself, his thoughts and feelings as something separated from the rest, a kind of optical delusion of his consciousness. This delusion is a kind of prison for us, restricting us to our personal desires and to affection for a few persons nearest to us. Our task must be to free ourselves from this prison by widening our circle of compassion to embrace all living creatures and the whole of nature in its beauty.[6]

• PART 4 •

LIVING ON THE BRINK

16

THE PSYCHOLOGICAL IMPACT OF
THREATS TO HUMAN SURVIVAL

Each of us is called on to do something that no member of any generation before ours has had to do: to assume responsibility for the continuation of our kind—to choose human survival. . . . For the risk of extinction is not just one more item on the agenda of issues that face us. Embracing, as it does, the life and death of every human being on earth and every future human being, it embraces and transcends all other issues.

—Jonathan Schell

Our old ways of thinking and acting have brought us to an evolutionary crossroads. We face the distinct possibility of our individual and collective extinction. This possibility has an impact on everything in our lives in ways both obvious and subtle, immediate and far-reaching. It is a time of great stress and challenge, risk and opportunity, of potential regression or evolution. Which it will be may determine our fate, and which it will be is a choice for which we must take responsibility.

As the old saying goes, "Life will either grind you down or polish you up," and which it does is now our choice. On one hand, we may respond with an exacerbation of the fear, defensiveness, and aggression that created our dilemma, and thereby regress in even more dangerous ways. On the other, we may use the situation to spur ourselves to rethink our values and choices, to explore and resolve the psychological dynamics with which we endangered ourselves, and thereby accelerate our individual and cultural maturation. Never in the course of human history have the stakes been higher.

NEGATIVE PSYCHOLOGICAL EFFECTS

What, then, are the negative psychological effects that these threats create?

As yet, research on these complications has been limited to the nuclear threat. These studies make very clear the fact that nuclear issues have deeply touched both adults and children. A significant number of both American and Soviet children expect a nuclear war within their lifetimes, doubt that they will survive, and report feelings of anger, impotence, and despair.[1] Some people who felt endangered by the accident at the Three Mile Island nuclear power plant still complained of stress a year later.[2] When it is remembered how relatively minor that accident was, the psychological consequences of nuclear war become inconceivable. Even the passage of four decades has not ended the suffering of those who survived Hiroshima and Nagasaki.[3]

Research on the psychological effects of other global threats is minimal. Pollution can cause a number of psychological problems, but as yet we do not have detailed information about the impact of these other threats.

Some of these effects must be catastrophic. The massive life-threatening stresses faced each day by hundreds of millions in the Third World probably exact psychological costs on a scale quite unknown to those of us living in developed countries. It is hard to imagine the anguish of not only facing starvation and preventable disease oneself, but also of watching one's children die needlessly. Such experiences probably create not only individual psychopathology but also resentment, violence, and social breakdown.

The same psychological defenses, distortions, and inauthenticities that contribute *to* global crises may also result *from* them. For as stresses mount, so also does the temptation to resort to defensiveness and inauthenticity. Yet denial, repression, or other defenses are always purchased at the cost of awareness, authenticity, and effectiveness. When we deny reality we also deny our full potential and humanity. When we distort our image of the world we distort our image of ourselves. When we fear to look out at the world we fear to look into ourselves. Therefore we remain unaware of the power and potential that lie within us and are us; the power and potential that are the major resources we have to offer to the world. In short, the costs of being unwilling to know the world truly are not knowing, and underestimating, ourselves.

Here then are the makings of yet another vicious cycle. For it is our sense of inadequacy and vulnerability that causes us to erect defenses and behave unskillfully in the first place. Yet these help create the global problems that in turn tempt us to greater defensiveness. As at the individual level, so also at the global: defenses create what they were designed to defend against.

To this already tragic cycle may be added the deadly burden of guilt. For no matter how desperately we defend ourselves, our defenses are never completely successful. Sooner or later there must filter past our well-guarded barriers the recognition of how privileged we are by comparison with so many others, and how unskillful are so many of our responses to the world's pain. With these recognitions comes the temptation of guilt. The guilt of failed idealism arises as we recognize that we have not met our own standards. "Survivor guilt" arises as we acknowledge the unfairness of a world in which we survive while millions of people, no less sensitive, human, and deserving of happiness than ourselves, suffer and die.

Guilt always seeks someone to blame and is not particularly fussy about who it is. If ourselves, we condemn and denigrate ourselves, thereby exacerbating the unworthiness and inadequacy that started the whole mess. If others, we look for people to scapegoat. These people may even include the victims themselves when we fall prey to the so-called "fair world syndrome." Here we attempt to rationalize and justify their suffering by arguing that the fault lies with the laziness, incompetence, or stupidity of the victims themselves. Here is yet another place where forgiveness, of both ourselves and others, is crucial.

In summary, as long as we are unwilling to look honestly at the world and ourselves then our responses to the world's problems will increase those very actions and defenses that created the problems in the first place.

POSSIBLE BENEFICIAL EFFECTS

On the other hand, these threats may also afford us great opportunities. Great threats call forth great responses. History is filled with stories of human greatness in times of danger and despair. Concentration camps, for example, have always been known, not only as the death place of bodies, but also as the birthplace of the highest flowerings of the human spirit; of extraordinary courage, compassion, and sacrifice, and of remarkable psychological growth, philosophical reflection, and religious inspiration.[4]

Might our current global threats do likewise? Might they also call forth the greatness and potential that lie within us all? Perhaps today's unprecedented threats may call us to more thoughtful living and greater contribution. If we choose to let them, they might strip away our defenses and help us to confront both the true condition of the world and our role in creating it. They might call us to examine our lives and values with new urgency and depth, and to open ourselves fully, perhaps for the first time, to the fundamental questions of our existence.

This opening, this willingness to question, to see the world and ourselves as we really are, may be vital to both our survival and to our psychological well-being. For to open ourselves fully to these fundamental issues of life is not only one of the hallmarks of psychological health, but also one of its causes.[5] For when we are willing to recognize the reality of our own mortality, of the enormity of preventable suffering in the world, of the rampant inhumanity, greed, hatred, delusion, and defensiveness, and of the precarious existence of ourselves, our families, and our fellow humans, then we are moved to question and reflect. Then we are open to explore at new and deeper levels the meaning, purpose, and appropriateness of our lifestyles, relationships, values, and personal and national goals. As has been pointed out by religious sages for centuries and more recently by psychologists, to the extent we confront these issues honestly and fully, to that extent will we mature and contribute. For such confrontations are likely to evoke the recognition of the fragility and preciousness of life, of our shared humanity, of the many ways in which we have been unconscious, unthinking, and insensitive, and of how, in the depths of our hearts, we really want to live with awareness and ethicality, compassion and contribution.[6]

Such responses tend to flow automatically from a willingness to see things as they truly are. For to see the extent of needless suffering in the world is also to feel compassion; to see the cost of our defensiveness is to desire to let it go; to see what our lifestyles really do to the planet is to want to live with greater sensitivity. "Awareness per se—by and of itself—can be curative."[7] To see things and ourselves as we really are! This is a crucial means for psychological growth and well-being of individuals and for the well-being and survival of our planet.

Such psychological growth is highly desirable, perhaps even vital to our survival. Remember that psychological immaturity is one of the central causes of our dilemma, and so survival may well depend on individual and social maturation. If we are to survive, it may be that we will have to call forth new depths of ingenuity and wisdom, cooperation and compassion, altruism and acceptance. Likewise, our survival may be dependent on unprecedented relinquishments of attack and defensiveness, selfishness and materialism, competition and consumption. For it may be that we will either live together as mature adults or die together as selfish, squabbling children. The only alternative to noncooperation may be nonexistence.

THE CALL TO SERVICE

The only ones among you who will be truly happy are those who have sought and found how to serve.

Albert Schweitzer

One other healthy response that might be expected is an increased amount of contribution and service. Considerable research indicates that psychologically healthy people tend to be particularly concerned for the welfare of others.[8] It follows that if we do manage our current dilemma with maturing responses, then these responses will include greater compassion and contribution.

However, increasing numbers of people may be moved to action and contribution whether or not significant degrees of psychological maturation occur. Indeed, one of the most hopeful signs is the rapidly growing number of people responding to global problems. Ecology, social responsibility, voluntary simplicity, nuclear freeze: these are no longer vague underground movements but visible and growing forces for planetary preservation. Probably half of all the books on ecology have been published in the last ten years; half of the books on nuclear weapons in the last five. In 1983 a majority of

United States citizens listed nuclear war as the foremost problem confronting the country. In just six years, over two million people joined the Hunger Project, a group committed to the elimination of starvation by the year 2000. The list is long and expanding, and the trend is heartening: global threats appear to be evoking increasing concern and contributions from more and more people. The race between contribution and catastrophe is on.

Obviously we need contributions of all kinds: letter-writing, education, public speaking, media presentations, publishing, political lobbying, donations, and more. But inasmuch as the fundamental problem is psychological, then we especially need people who not only do these things, but who also do them with deep understanding of the underlying psychological principles and issues.

Therefore, we need people who commit themselves to two types of service. The first is to the symptomatic relief of suffering in the world. The second is to psychological awareness, both their own and that of others, to relieve the mental causes of this suffering and to make themselves more effective. For as Jerome Frank and many others have pointed out time and time again, "We have to start with changes within ourselves."[9] The most far-reaching social and global transformations must all start in the same place: within ourselves. Therefore, "If you are serious about the sufferings of mankind, you must perfect the only source of help you have—yourself."[10]

If we need this kind of two-pronged approach in the world and on ourselves then it would make sense to combine them. It would make sense to approach our work in such a way that we learn and grow from it. This approach has been used in many forms of service, but the classic example is the millenia old Eastern tradition of karma yoga. This is the discipline of service and work in the world, in which that service and work are viewed as opportunities for learning and awakening. The aim is impeccable service that simultaneously relieves suffering and also awakens self and others. In doing so, it aims at inclusive treatment of both symptom and cause, self and other, psyche and world.

People using this approach go into themselves in order to go more effectively out into the world and go out into the world in order to go deeper into themselves. The deeper this exploration and the greater their psychological understanding, the more they are able to appreciate that many of the psychological factors causing our crises stem from widely accepted cultural beliefs, values, and behaviors. Therefore, to be most effective, these people must work toward extracting themselves from limiting and distorting cultural biases. This is the process of "detribalization," by which a person matures from an ethnocentric to a global world view; from "my country, right or wrong" to "our planet"; and from identification with a group or nation to identification with humankind. Such a person develops "perspectivism"—the capacity to see other peoples' points of view—and becomes "less dependent upon tribal rewards, more questioning of tribal values, more able to look on life from a universalistic perspective."[11] The result is that the person is no longer blinded by cultural biases, but rather recognizes them for what they are and hence can work on them to effect change.[12]

17

AN EVOLUTIONARY PERSPECTIVE

We are compelled to rethink what life means and where we wish to go. We are obliged to sort out the trivial from the significant, the ephemeral from the durable, and to find an alternative image of human and social possibility that captures our collective imagination and provides a renewed sense of direction.

—Duane Elgin

We have created a world situation that appears to demand unprecedented psychological and social maturation for our survival. Until now we have been able to cover or compensate for our psychological shortcomings. We have been able to consume without fear of depletion, discard wastes without fear of pollution, bear children without fear of overpopulation, and fight without fear of extinction. We have been able to act out our psychological immaturities rather than having to understand and outgrow them, to indulge our addictions rather than resolve them, and to revolve through the same neurotic patterns rather than evolve out of them. But if all the world is a stage, it is now no longer a big enough one for us to continue playing out our psychological immaturities. It is time for us to grow up, and we ourselves have created the situation that may force us to do so.

This growing up that is demanded of us, this psychological maturation, this development of consciousness, is a form of evolution. For evolution is of both bodies and minds, of matter and consciousness.[1] "Evolution is an ascent towards consciousness," wrote Teilhard de Chardin, a view that has been echoed by Eastern thinkers such as Aurobindo, who thought that "evolution of consciousness is the central motive of terrestrial existence" and that our next evolutionary step would be "a change of consciousness."[2]

Moreover, this evolution is of a new kind. For it is conscious evolution; a conscious choosing of our future, driven by necessity but steered by choice.[3] "Man occupies the crest of the evolutionary wave," said Aurobindo.[4] "With him occurs the passage from an unconscious to a conscious evolution." This is not only evolution but the evolution of evolution.

Because it demands greater development and maturation of us, our

81

global crisis may therefore function as an evolutionary catalyst. Necessity may be not only the mother of invention but also of evolution.

This gives us a very, very different view of our situation. For from this perspective our current crisis can be seen not as an unmitigated disaster but as an evolutionary challenge, not just as a pull to regression and extinction but as a push to new evolutionary heights. It can be seen as a call to each and every one of us, both individually and collectively, to become and contribute as much as we can. This perspective gives us both a vision of the future and a motive for working toward it.

But, it might be argued, is not this image idealistic? Yes, indeed it is! But this is by no means bad. For on one hand our situation seems to demand nothing less than this, and on the other, idealistic images can be very helpful if used skillfully.

Unfortunately, our usual use of ideals is far from skillful. On the one hand we tend to regard them as hopelessly unattainable and either scoff or give up in despair. On the other we use them as excuses for punishing ourselves whenever we do not attain them. Either approach is a good way of ensuring ourselves more pain.

But there is a more skillful way of using ideals. This is to see them not just as goals that must be reached, but also as guiding images or visions that provide signposts and directions for our lives and decisions. Such images attract us to actualize them and ourselves.

This is the way in which we need to view the evolutionary image of our current situation and the developmental advances it might elicit. It is crucial that we not automatically dismiss them as hopelessly idealistic. Rather, we need to see them as possibilities offering guidance and direction for escaping our current quandary and for realizing our potentials as both individuals and as a species.

This challenge of individual maturation and evolutionary advance may be one of the most fulfilling tasks we can undertake. For this pull to greater awareness, to actualize our full potential, and to transcend our present limits may be a major human motive. So at least think humanistic, transpersonal, Jungian, Eastern, and certain existential psychologists. "The basic actualizing tendency is the only motive which is postulated in this system," said the great humanistic psychologist Carl Rogers.[5]

To fulfill this desire may therefore be deeply rewarding. Failing to fulfill it, on the other hand, may result not only in a failure of growth, but in a particular kind of psychological suffering, a kind which often goes unrecognized. For when these actualizing needs go ungratified their effects are subtle, existential, and therefore less easily identified. "In general, they have been discussed through the centuries by religionists, historians, and philosophers under the rubric of spiritual or religious shortcomings, rather than by physicians, scientists, or psychologists," said Abraham Maslow.[6] He called them "metapathologies," and described such examples as alienation, meaningless-ness, and cynicism, as well as various existential, philosophical, and religious crises. Yet these are the very symptoms that have plagued Western societies increasingly in recent decades[7] and which contribute to the growing sense of social unrest. In other words, the very immaturities and failures of psycho-logical growth from which stem our global crises may also be central to the prevailing psychological malaise of our time.

A perspective that sees our global crisis as a potential evolutionary cata-lyst may therefore help in several ways. Research shows that when people face a life-threatening crisis they feel a desperate need to restore their self-esteem by attempting to regain mastery of the situation and finding some sense of meaning in it.[8]

An evolutionary view meets these needs well. It provides a sense of mean-ing on a grand scale; a scale that encompasses the totality of contemporary threats, includes individuals and the entire species, and transcends all tradi-tional national and political boundaries. It enhances self-esteem by seeing our current situation not as final proof of human inadequacy and futility, but rather as a self-created challenge speeding us on our evolutionary journey. It motivates us to regain mastery of the situation and in the process demands that we fulfill our individual and collective potential far more than at any time in history. It also provides an antidote to the metapathologies of purpose-lessness and alienation that have haunted developed countries during recent decades.

By their own theories of human nature, psychologists have the power of elevat-ing or degrading that same nature. Debasing assumptions debase human be-ings; generous assumptions exalt them.[9]

An evolutionary perspective appears to provide a meaningful and inspir-ing view of our contemporary predicament and to exalt human nature at the same time.

Such a perspective is also similar to those that have developed at other times of great transformation. Analysis of the few truly major transformations of human self-image throughout history suggest that they have all included a broad-ranging synthesis of knowledge and an evolutionary view of human-kind.[10] The first order of business for humanity, said the great thinkers such as Plato and Thomas Aquinas who sparked these transformations, is to align ourselves with this evolution.

But where is this evolution taking us? What is our destiny in the uni-verse? To answer this is to go beyond objective facts and to state our personal philosophy, our faith, and our world view.

The two extremes are probably represented by materialism and "the perennial philosophy," the central core of understanding common to the great religions. To the materialist perspective, life and consciousness are accidental by-products of matter, and their evolution is driven by the interplay of random events and the instinct for survival. The purpose of human life and evolution is solely what humanity decides it is.

The perennial philosophy, which lies at the heart of the great religions and is increasingly said to represent their deepest thinking,[11] suggests a very different view. It views consciousness as central and its development as the primary goal of existence. This development is said to culminate in the condition variously known in different traditions as enlightenment, liberation, salvation, *moksha*, or *satori*.

The descriptions of this condition show remarkable similarities across cultures and centuries.[12] Its essence is said to be the recognition that the distortions of our usual state of mind are such that we have been suffering from a case of mistaken identity. Our true nature is said to be something much greater, an aspect of a universal consciousness: Self, Being, Mind, or God. The awakening to this true nature, claimed a Zen master, is "the direct awareness that you are more than this puny body or limited mind. Stated negatively, it is the realization that the universe is not external to you. Positively, it is experiencing the universe as yourself."[13] Similar descriptions could be found in almost any culture. Typical is the claim by an Englishman that to realize our true identity is to "find that the I, one's real, most intimate self, pervades the universe and all other beings. That the mountains, and the sea, and the stars are a part of one's body, and that one's soul is in touch with the souls of all creatures."[14] Nor are such descriptions the exclusive province of mystics. They have been echoed by philosophers, psychologists, and physicists.[15] "Out of my experience . . . one final conclusion dogmatically emerges," said the great American philosopher William James. "There is a continuum of cosmic consciousness against which our individuality builds but accidental forces, and into which our several minds plunge as into a mother sea."[16]

From this perspective evolution is a vast journey of growing self-awareness and return to our true identity.[17] Our current crises are seen as expressions of the mistaken desires, fears, and perceptions that arise from our mistaken identity. But they can also be seen as self-created challenges that may speed us on our evolutionary journey toward ultimate self recognition.

Which world view is correct? Are we solely survival-driven animals or are we also awakening gods? How can we decide? Both world views give answers that are similar and different: similar in that they both tell us to research and explore, different in what they tell us to explore. For the world view of materialism says to explore the physical universe and thereby ourselves; the perennial philosophy says to explore our own minds and consciousness and thereby the universe. "Know thyself" is its central credo.

But in practical terms it seems crucial that we do both. Our survival and evolution require no less than that we deepen our understanding of both the universe within and the universe without.

Whichever world view we adopt, then, still allows us to see our contemporary crossroads as an evolutionary challenge calling us to choose and create our destiny. That challenge asks of us that we relinquish our former limits and be and become and contribute all that we can. It calls us to play our full part in the unfolding human drama that we ourselves have created and asks that we choose, both individually and collectively, conscious evolution.

In conclusion, hard material necessity and human evolutionary possibility now seem to converge to create a situation where, in the long run, we will be obliged to do no less than realize our greatest possibilities. We are engaged in a race between self-discovery and self-destruction. The forces that may converge to destroy us are the same forces that may foster societal and self-discovery.[18]

18

"WHAT CAN I DO?"

There is no one who can take our place. Each of us weaves a strand in the web of creation. There is no one who can weave that strand for us. What we have to contribute is both unique and irreplaceable. What we withhold from life is lost to life. The entire world depends upon our individual choices.

—Duane Elgin

What can I do? This is what it ultimately comes down to. After we have given up blaming others for our difficulties, after we have stopped hoping for some mythical savior or white knight, and after we have relinquished our sense of inadequacy and impotence, then we ask, "What can I do?"

But there is a still more important question we can ask. This is not only, "What can I do?" but also, "What is the most strategic thing I can do?" Therefore, our first task is to look for ways in which our contributions can have optimal impact; the ways in which the talents and opportunities that are uniquely ours can be put to best use.

The first step, then, is simply to reflect deeply and carefully on our life situation. We need to examine our desires and find the answer to, "What would I really like to do?" Here it is important to set aside the tyrannical self orders about what we *should* do, the limiting beliefs about what we *cannot* do, and first simply find what we would *like* to do. It is important to recognize that doing things out of guilt or "shoulds" is counterproductive. Such motivation spawns anger, tension, and righteousness with which you will infect other people. This is hardly helpful since emotions such as these are part of the problem and our task is to reduce them.

That is why it is so important to learn a little-known secret about contribution and service: it is okay to have a good time. All too often we approach service with grim-faced determination and a hidden assumption that we are not really serious about it if we are not suffering. Yes, it is true the world is in bad shape, but creating more suffering in ourselves is hardly the way to relieve it.

So our first task is to look for the strategic contributions that we might like to make. Talking with people can be very helpful, but so too can periods of solitude and quiet. When Gandhi was wrestling with the question of how best to respond to the British tax on salt and the law forbidding Indians from taking the free and plentiful salt lying on every beach, he went into retirement for weeks. After many, many days of quiet reflection and prayer the strategic answer finally came. He set off across India walking toward the ocean to take some salt. News of his pilgrimage spread, and his journey was widely reported. After many days he finally reached the shore, stooped down, picked up a single handful of salt, and as millions followed his example the British empire and its salt laws were sent reeling.

Strategic responses require information, of course, and so self-education about our problems and their causes is essential. Tragically enough, simply reading this book will make you better informed about these matters than many people in government.

From this education and reflection you will gradually become aware of the responses that feel right for you. These might usefully include any traditional approach such as organizing groups, lobbying and writing to those in power, educating others, donating or raising money, writing or public speaking, and more.

But the challenge for all of us is also to create new approaches that fit our particular talents and situations; approaches that reach new people and that have an impact in novel ways. What would Gandhi do if he lived at this time in your unique situation? How would he go about looking for the most strategic contribution he could make, and what would it be? Here is a challenge for creativity and a game worth playing.

PSYCHOLOGICAL UNDERSTANDING

There is another whole aspect to this game of strategic contribution, and that is its psychological side. We have been discussing what we can do, but equally important is how we do it. When we remember how crucial are the psychological causes of our difficulties then it becomes obvious that whatever we do should take this into consideration. The question now becomes this: "How do I approach whatever I do in a way that reduces the psychological causes of global problems and enhances psychological awareness and maturation in people, including myself?" In other words, "How do I practice and apply the psychological principles discussed in this book?"

The first step is a shift in attitude, a change in the way we approach our work, our world, and ourselves. It involves bringing to everything we do a desire to learn and grow. Every experience is viewed as a potential source of learning about the world, other people, and ourselves. We explore both the world outside us and the world within us, learning from our subjective experience, our hopes, fears, thoughts, and emotions, as much as from events outside us. To each thing we experience or do we bring as much careful attention and awareness as we can.

Once we have begun to adopt this attitude, then other people and all our experiences become a kind of feedback. If something we do works well, we explore it to learn why. If we make a mistake (which we will, repeatedly: it is part of being human), we explore it also. If we hold this perspective then there is no need for regrets and recriminations; these are sorry substitutes for learning. Our mistakes can ultimately prove as valuable as our triumphs, sometimes even more so.

As we slowly learn to bring greater sensitivity and awareness to all that we do, we become aware of the mistaken beliefs, perceptions, and actions that limit us and our ability to contribute. As we recognize them, then we learn from and relinquish them. If we find limiting beliefs such as "I can't do that," or "I could never . . ." we simply recognize them as mere beliefs, and belittling ones at that, and go right ahead to do what we formerly thought was beyond us. If we notice ourselves condemning and attacking people, including ourselves, we learn from that, finding the causes of our anger, and noticing its costs. Perhaps this condemnation will go further to seeing other people as "the enemy." If so, we would want to recognize our dualistic thinking and look for the areas of common experience and purpose we share with this "enemy." It may also be skillful to recognize their fear and defensiveness and to try to forgive rather than attack them.

If we become fearful and defensive ourselves, which being human we will, we have an opportunity to learn how these emotions affect our minds. We will also get a chance to understand the addiction and insecurities from which they spring. From this understanding can come empathy and compassion for those who are dominated by fear and defensiveness and who attack and destroy because of them.

When we are tempted to be dishonest and unethical we can become aware of the costs of guilt and paranoia in ourselves and of the pain brought to others. However, it is important that this awareness is cultivated, not to condemn and punish ourselves, but to learn and grow.

As we cultivate awareness and make our contributions, we will soon see that we are addicted to having certain things happen. Perhaps we want praise and recognition or crave anonymity, perhaps we must have our ideas accepted, or perhaps we must always lead or always follow.

Almost all of us will find some addiction to having our contributions produce the results we want. This certainly seems a reasonable enough goal, which it is, but when we become addicted to it the result is sure to be trouble. For now we have said, "I *must* get my way," and we have set ourselves up to experience frustration and disappointment as well as anger at those who block us. Remember that many of the people creating our global crises are doing so because they are addicted to their particular solutions, whether those solutions be communism, capitalism, more resource usage, or nuclear weapons.

That is why it is so important to remember that even our best intentions can be mistaken.

It is also why it is crucial that we reduce our addictions, even those addictions to the successful outcomes of our contributions. For as we reduce these addictions we also reduce our egocentric viewpoint, our fears of failure, and our resentment at those who block us. The result is greater equanimity, clarity, and effectiveness, since our vision is now less distorted by egocentric desires and fears. Last, but hardly least, we also feel happier.

Once we have reached this stage we can use our suffering as feedback that we are addicted to things being a particular way. For psychological pain is like physical pain, a signal that something is wrong. If we respond only by trying to change the world then we maintain our addictions and suffer again the next time they are not gratified. But if we work to change the world *and* reduce our addictions then we are healing both psyche and world, self and other.

The more awareness we bring to bear, the more everything becomes part of our learning. Everything we do and experience becomes a means of deepening our understanding. Everything becomes a means of reducing our addictions and aversions, of cultivating empathy and compassion, of accepting and forgiving, and of becoming more effective learners and contributors. Our lives have become learning laboratories in which we are both experimenter and subject, teacher and student, server and served.

LIFESTYLE

With increasing awareness and understanding we may begin to notice ways in which our lifestyles conflict both with what we truly want and with what would be ecologically appropriate. Though once hidden under the veils of insensitivity and unconsciousness, these discrepancies become increasingly obtrusive and nag at us for correction. For as we examine them and ourselves we find that many of these discrepancies reflect addictions, fears, and other psychological errors similar to those that create our global problems.

These lifestyle discrepancies can take many forms. Perhaps we are buying, consuming, and discarding without regard for ecological impact. For example, perhaps we are using heat instead of insulation, a car even though good public transportation is available, or nonreusable goods rather than reusable ones. Perhaps we are making ourselves and our family anxious and tense by overworking to earn extra money for things that we do not really need. Perhaps we are working for or investing in an industry that is harming the environment, creating dangerous products, or taking unfair advantage of underdeveloped countries. Perhaps we are buying from companies that sponsor particularly violent television programming or are not expressing our appreciation to sponsors and stations that show educational programs about global problems. Perhaps we could donate more of our time or money to the causes that inspire us. As Duane Elgin points out:

Opportunities for meaningful and important action are everywhere: the food that we choose to eat, the work that we choose to do, the transportation we choose to use, the manner in which we choose to relate to others, the clothing that we choose to wear, the learning that we choose to acquire, the compassionate causes that we choose to support, the level of attention that we choose to give to our moment-to-moment passage through life, and on and on. The list is endless since the stuff of social transformation is identical with the stuff from which our daily lives are made.[1]

WITHDRAWAL AND RETURN

With time the costs of our psychological foibles and the benefits of cultivating learning, awareness, and growth become increasingly obvious. As they do so we may feel a growing need to set aside time devoted specifically to our own healing, learning, and maturing. Such time is not selfish; it is vital both for our own well-being and for our ability to contribute.

Sadly enough, this fact is rarely appreciated even though many wise people have echoed it for many years. "Finding the center of strength within ourselves is in the long run the best contribution we can make to our fellow men," said the existentialist Rollo May,[2] thereby echoing the words of the Buddha, who argued that "to straighten the crooked, you must first do a harder thing—straighten yourself."[3] For this reason:

It is a grave error to accuse a man who pursues self-knowledge of "turning his back on society." The opposite would be more nearly true: that a man who fails to pursue self-knowledge is and remains a danger to society, for he will tend to misunderstand everything that other people say or do, and remain blissfully unaware of the significance of many of the things he does himself.[4]

So crucial is this phase of inner exploration and work that it has been found in the lives of most of the truly great contributors to humankind. It has also been embodied in heroic myths across centuries and cultures. The great historian Arnold Toynbee named it "the law of withdrawal and return."[5] It was described in a review of the lives of great heroes, both real and mythical, as follows:

In a word: the first work of the hero is to retreat from the world scene of secondary effects to those causal zones of the psyche where the difficulties really reside, and there to clarify the difficulties and eradicate them in his own case.[6]

91

We may not all be world heroes, but we can certainly learn from their example. How then can we best facilitate our "retreat to the causal zones of the psyche" and our clarification of the difficulties? What environment and people will allow us to dip most deeply into our psychic resources and tap the strength and healing powers that lie there?

This is an individual question that each of us must ask and answer for ourselves. For some the answer might be that we need a period of solitude and quiet; for others it might be that we could benefit from spending more time with family or friends. Some of us may find greatest insight and inspiration in nature, others may find periods of time spent in quiet reflection, contemplation, prayer, or meditation to be particularly helpful. At times we may benefit from groups or workshops with people working on similar issues. But whatever we feel will be most helpful to our learning and well-being, it is important that we give ourselves the time to do it.

When we have done this and feel ready, we can go out into the world again. As we do we bring with us the gifts of understanding, calm, and renewed energy won during the time of withdrawal. In the world we make our contributions as strategically as we can, removing misunderstanding and suffering as best we can. As the inevitable frustrations, defenses, and resentments begin to mount, we work to understand and reduce them as they arise but also honor the need for periodic withdrawal.

As the cycle of withdrawal and return continues the distinction between what benefits us and what benefits others becomes more and more transparent. Each contribution becomes a learning opportunity, each learning becomes an opportunity for greater contributions. As the boundary between what benefits us and what benefits others becomes thinner, then egocentric desires, fears, and comparisons diminish, and the boundary between us and others also grows thinner. Gradually we look past the veils of separation and otherness and recognize our shared humanity. And as we do, the words of an ancient Indian proverb begin to make sense:

When I do not know who I am I serve you.
When I know who I am I am you.

At this point the psychological causes of our global crises have been reduced within ourselves. For without "others" there is no cause for fear, paranoia, and defensiveness on the one hand, and on the other, responses of empathy and compassion arise spontaneously.[7] Our cycle of withdrawal and return, of work in the world and in ourselves, has reached fruition, and the question, "What can I do?" has been answered.

This, then, is one form of service and contribution. It is a form recommended across centuries by both the great growth disciplines and the great religions and can be viewed either psychologically or religiously as one chooses. "Seek, above all, for a game worth playing," is the advice of certain psychologists. "Having found the game, play it with intensity—play as if your life and sanity depended on it. (They do depend on it.)"[8] Conscious, choiceful contribution and learning is a game worth playing, and the fate of the earth may depend on the number of people who elect to play it.

We are called to a task greater than that demanded of any generation in human history: to preserve our planet and our species. In accepting this challenge we are also called to recognize, develop, and redirect the awesome power of our minds, and to consciously choose and create our evolution.

Never in the course of human history has the need been greater. Never in the course of human history have so many people needlessly suffered and died. Never in the course of human history have so many hungered and been oppressed. And never have so many lives (some five billion) hung in the balance.

And never in the course of human history have the opportunities been greater. Never have we had such powerful resources and technologies available to relieve the world's suffering. Never has there been such potential for developing a global psychology to understand the motives and behaviors that threaten us, and those that may yet save us. The magnitude of our difficulties may be matched only by the magnitude of our opportunities.

There may, therefore, be no more urgent or rewarding task facing each and every one of us than to acknowledge and fulfill our role in creating and applying a psychology of human survival and a psychology linking all those from all nations who wish to apply their skills to these, the most urgent issues of our time, unveiling the psychological forces that have brought us to this turning point in history, and working to transform them into forces for our collective survival, well-being, and evolution. There is exciting and desperately needed work to be done, and we are privileged to have the opportunity of doing it.

CHAPTER NOTES

CHAPTER 1

1. M. Ferguson, *The Aquarian Conspiracy* (Los Angeles: J. P. Tarcher, 1979); and C. Reich, *The Greening of America* (New York: Random House, 1970).

2. E. Ericksen, "A Developmental Crisis of Mankind," talk presented at Physicians for Social Responsibility meeting, Stanford University, October 1983.

3. F. Capra, *The Turning Point* (New York: Simon & Schuster, 1982).

4. W. Davidson, "Psychiatry and Foreign Affairs," *Psychiatric Annals* 13 (1983): 124.

CHAPTER 2

1. B. Wedge, "Peacemaking," *Psychiatric Annals* 13 (1983): 136.

2. A. H. Maslow, *Toward a Psychology of Being*, 2nd ed. (Princeton: Van Nostrand, 1968).

3. Council on Environmental Quality, *The Global 2000 Report to the President* (Washington, D.C.: U.S. Government Printing Office, 1979). Other analyses include the World Integrated Model, the United Nations' Model, and the Latin American World Model. They are all in general agreement, except for the *Global 2000 Revised* study (H. Kahn and J. Simon, 1984, forthcoming), which paints a more optimistic but also more questionable picture.

4. Council on Environmental Quality, 7.

5. Council on Environmental Quality and Population Reference Bureau, *Annual Report* (Washington, D.C.: Population Reference Bureau, 1983).

6. National Academy of Sciences, *Resources and Man* (San Francisco: Freeman, 1969), 5.

7. E. Dammann, *The Future in Our Hands* (New York: Pergamon, 1979), 104.

8. R. Ayres, *Banking on the Poor: The World Bank and World Poverty* (Cambridge, Mass.: MIT Press, 1983); and J. Loup, *Can the Third World Survive?* (Baltimore: Johns Hopkins University Press, 1983).

9. W. Brandt, *North South: A Program for Survival* (Cambridge, Mass.: MIT Press, 1980).

10. R. Sivard, *World Military and Social Expenditures* (Leesburg, Va.: World Priorities, 1979).

11. P. Mische, *State of the World: A Global Agenda* (Los Angeles: Franciscan Communications, 1981).

12. Dammann, *The Future in Our Hands*, 91.

13. Presidential Commission on World Hunger, *Preliminary Report of the Presidential Commission on World Hunger* (Washington, D.C.: U.S. Government Printing Office, 1979).

14. C. Paine, "The Aftermath of Nuclear War," *Science* 220 (1983): 812.

15. World Bank, *World Development Report* (Washington, D. C.: U. S. Government Printing Office, 1979).

16. Ponnamperuma, "First Word," *Omni* 5:9 (1983): 6.

17. H. Henderson, *The Politics of the Solar Age* (Garden City, N. Y.: Anchor/Doubleday, 1981).

18. Ayres, *Banking on the Poor*; and Loup, *Can the Third World Survive?*

19. World Bank, *World Development Report*.

20. Council on Environmental Quality, *The Global 2000 Report*, 32.

21. Ibid.

22. G. Woodwell et al., "Global Deforestation: Contribution to Atmospheric Carbon Dioxide," *Science* 222 (1983): 1081–1086.

23. L. Brown, *Building a Sustainable Society* (New York: W. W. Norton, 1981); and L. Brown, *State of the World* (New York: W. W. Norton, 1984).

24. R. H. Boyle and R. A. Boyle, *Acid Rain* (New York: Schocken Books, 1983).

25. R. Kerr, "The Carbon Cycle and Climate Warming," *Science* 222 (1983): 1107–1108; and Woodwell et al., "Global Deforestation."

26. Council on Environmental Quality, *The Global 2000 Report*; National Academy of Sciences, *Report of the Carbon Dioxide Assessment Committee* (Washington, D.C.: National Academy Press, 1983); and S. Seidel and D. Keyes, *Can We Delay a Greenhouse Warming?* (Washington, D.C.: U.S. Government Printing Office, 1983).

27. R. McNamara, Address to the Board of Governors of the World Bank, Belgrade, 2 Oct. 1979.

28. Dammann, *The Future in Our Hands*, 46.

CHAPTER 3

1. R. Sivard, *World Military and Social Expenditures* (Leesburg, Va.: World Priorities, 1983).

2. J. Schell, *The Fate of the Earth* (New York: Knopf, 1982).

3. P. Bracken, *The Command and Control of Nuclear Forces* (New Haven: Yale University Press, 1983).

4. B. Bereanu, "Self Activation of the World Nuclear Weapons System," *Journal of Peace Research* 20 (1983): 49-57.

5. D. Barash and J. Lipton, *Stop Nuclear War: A Handbook* (New York: Grove, 1982).

6. J. Steinbruner, "Launch Under Attack," *Scientific American* 250 (1984): 37-47.

7. T. Onosko, "Showdown on the High Frontier," *Omni* 6:2 (1983): 80.

8. Barash and Lipton, *Stop Nuclear War*.

9. L. Carter, "WIPP Goes Ahead, Amid Controversy," *Science* 222 (1983): 1102–1104.

10. H. Caldicott, *Nuclear Madness: What You Can Do* (Brookline, Mass.: Autumn Press, 1978).

11. Carter, "WIPP Goes Ahead."

12. Sivard, *World Military*.

13. C. Paine, "The Aftermath of Nuclear War," *Science* 220 (1983): 812.

14. Presidential Commission on World Hunger, *Preliminary Reports of the Presi-*

dential Commission on World Hunger (Washington, D.C.: U.S. Government Printing Office, 1979).

15. Barash and Lipton, *Stop Nuclear War*, 322.

16. B. Fuller, *Critical Path* (New York: St. Martin's Press, 1981).

17. K. Lewis, "The Prompt and Delayed Effects of Nuclear War," *Scientific American* 241, 1978: 35–47; Schell, *The Fate of the Earth*; and J. Schell, "The Abolition: Defining the Great Predicament," *The New Yorker*, January 1984: 36–75.

18. Paine, "The Aftermath."

19. L. Van Atta, "Arms Control: Human Control," *American Psychologist* 18 (1963): 39.

20. Schell, *The Fate of the Earth*.

21. R. Adams and S. Cullen, eds., *The Final Epidemic: Physicians and Scientists on Nuclear War* (Chicago: Educational Foundation for Nuclear Science, 1981); E. Chivian et al., eds., *Last Aid: The Medical Dimension of Nuclear War* (San Francisco: Freeman, 1982); Paine, "The Aftermath of Nuclear War"; and J. Peterson and D. Hinrichsen, eds., *Nuclear War: The Aftermath* (New York: Pergamon, 1982).

22. P. Ehrlich, J. Harte, and M. Harwell, "Long-Term Biological Consequences of Nuclear War," *Science* 222 (1983): 1293–1300; R. Turco et al., "Nuclear Winter: Global Consequences of Multiple Nuclear Explosions," *Science* 222 (1983): 1283–1292.

23. National Academy of Sciences, *Long-Term Worldwide Effects of Multiple Nuclear-Weapons Detonations* (Washington, D.C.: National Academy of Sciences, 1975).

24. J. Leaning and L. Keyes, eds., *The Counterfeit Ark* (Cambridge, Mass.: Ballinger, 1983).

25. Ehrlich et al., "Long-Term Biological Consequences," 1298.

26. Schell, *The Fate of the Earth*, 6.

27. L. Pressler, "First Word," *Omni* 6:2 (1983): 6.

28. Onosko, "Showdown," 80.

29. R. Garwin et al., "Antisatellite Weapons," *Scientific American* 250 (1984): 45–55; Union of Concerned Scientists, "Reagan's Star Wars," *New York Review of Books*, April 26, 1984.

30. Council on Environmental Quality, *The Global 2000 Report to the President* (Washington, D.C.: U.S. Government Printing Office, 1979), 3, 42.

CHAPTER 5

1. A. Bandura, "Self Efficacy: Toward a Unifying Theory of Behavioral Change," *Psychological Review* 84 (1977): 191–215; and R. Merton, *Social Theory and Social Structure* (Glencoe, Ill.: Free Press, 1957).

2. E. Langer, *The Psychology of Control* (Beverly Hills, Calif.: Sage, 1983); and R. Walsh, "Beyond Belief," *Journal of Humanistic Psychology* 1984.

3. E. F. Schumacher, *A Guide for the Perplexed* (New York: Harper & Row, 1977), 44.

4. R. Scheer, *With Enough Shovels: Reagan, Bush, and Nuclear War* (New York: Vintage, 1983).

5. *Time*, 2 Jan. 1984.

6. Ibid.

7. R. Lifton and R. Falk, *Indefensible Weapons: The Political and Psychological Case Against Nuclearism* (New York: Basic Books, 1982).

8. L. Brown, *Building a Sustainable Society* (New York: W. W. Norton, 1981).

CHAPTER 6

1. A. Bandura, *The Principles of Behavior Modification* (New York: Holt, Rinehart & Winston, 1969).

2. A. H. Maslow, *The Farther Reaches of Human Nature* (New York: Viking Press, 1971).

3. J. Galbraith, *The Anatomy of Power* (Boston: Houghton Mifflin, 1983).

4. R. Sivard, *World Military and Social Expenditures* (Leesburg, Va.: World Priorities, 1981).

5. H. Caldicott, *Nuclear Madness: What You Can Do* (Brookline, Mass.: Autumn Press, 1978).

6. D. Elgin, *Voluntary Simplicity* (New York: William Morrow, 1981).

7. E. Dammann, *The Future in Our Hands* (New York: Pergamon, 1979), 136.

8. D. Singer, "A Time to Reexamine the Role of Television in Our Lives," *American Psychologist* 38 (1983): 815–816.

9. D. Elgin, *The "Communications Rights" Movement: A New Response to National and Global Challenges* (Menlo Park, Calif.: Choosing Our Future, 1983), 15.

10. D. Pearl, L. Bouthilet, and J. Lazar, eds., *Television and Behavior: Ten Years of Scientific Progress and Implications for the Eighties*, vols. 1 and 2 (Washington, D.C.: U.S. Government Printing Office, 1982); and E. Rubinstein, "Television and Behavior: Research Conclusions of the 1982 NIMH Report and Their Policy Implications," *American Psychologist* 38 (1983): 820–825.

11. Elgin, *The "Communications Rights" Movement*; Galbraith, *The Anatomy of Power*; Rubinstein, "Television and Behavior"; Singer, "A Time to Reexamine"; and J. Singer and D. Singer, "Psychologists Look at Television: Cognitive, Developmental, Personality, and Social Policy Implications," *American Psychologist* 38 (1983): 826–834.

12. Elgin, *The "Communications Rights" Movement*.

CHAPTER 7

1. A. Deikman, *The Observing Self: Mysticism and Psychiatry* (Boston: Beacon Press, 1982); R. Walsh, "The Consciousness Disciplines and the Behavioral Sciences: Questions of Comparison and Assessment," *American Journal of Psychiatry* 137 (1980): 663–673; R. Walsh, *The Universe Within Us: New Understandings of Mind* (Forthcoming); K. Wilber, *The Spectrum of Consciousness* (Wheaton, Ill.: Quest, 1977); K. Wilber, *No Boundary* (Los Angeles: Center Press, 1979); K. Wilber, *A Sociable God: A Brief Introduction to a Transcendental Sociology* (New York: McGraw-Hill, 1983); and K. Wilber, *Eye to Eye: The Quest for the New Paradigm* (Garden City, N.Y.: Anchor/Doubleday, 1983).

2. E. Conze, *Buddhist Meditation* (New York: Harper & Row, 1975); D. Goleman, *The Varieties of the Meditative Experience* (New York: E. P. Dutton, 1977); and

Longchenpa, *Kindly Bent to Ease Us, Part I: Mind* (Emeryville, Calif.: Dharma, 1975).

3. A. Freedman, "Opiate Dependence," in *Comprehensive Textbook of Psychiatry*, eds. H. Kaplan, A. Freedman, and B. Sadock, 3rd ed., vol. 2 (Baltimore: Williams and Wilkins, 1980), 1591–1614; and J. Goldstein, *The Experience of Insight* (Boulder, Colo.: Shambhala, 1983).

4. Walsh, *The Universe Within Us*.

5. W. Harman, "Old Wine in New Wineskins," in *Challenges of Humanistic Psychology*, ed. J. Bugental (New York: McGraw-Hill, 1962), 323.

6. F. Perls, *Gestalt Therapy Verbatim* (Lafayette, Calif.: Real People Press, 1969), 124.

7. E. Langer, "Playing the Middle Against Both Ends: The Usefulness of Adult Cognitive Activity as a Model for Cognitive Activity in Childhood and Old Age," in *The Development of Reflection*, ed. S. Yussen (New York: Academic Press, 1982); E. Langer, A. Blank, and C. Benzion, "The Mindfulness of Ostensibly Thoughtful Action: The Role of 'Placebic' Information on Interpersonal Interaction," *Journal of Personality and Social Research* 36 (1978): 635–642; and E. Langer, *The Psychology of Control* (Beverly Hills, Calif.: Sage, 1983).

8. E. Becker, *The Denial of Death* (New York: Free Press, 1973), 24–30.

9. D. Brown, "A Model for the Levels of Concentrative Meditation," *International Journal of Clinical and Experimental Hypnosis* 25 (1977): 236–273; D. Brown and J. Engler, "The Stages of Mindfulness Meditation: A Validation Study," *Journal of Transpersonal Psychology* 12 (1980): 143–192; D. H. Shapiro, *Meditation: Self Regulation Strategy and Altered State of Consciousness* (New York: Aldine, 1980); D. H. Shapiro and R. Walsh, eds., *Meditation: Ancient and Contemporary Perspectives* (New York: Aldine, forthcoming); C. Tart, *States of Consciousness* (New York: Dutton, 1975); and C. Tart, ed., *Transpersonal Psychologies* (New York: Harper & Row, 1976).

10. American Psychological Association, *The Monitor* 14 (1983): 8.

11. Wilber, *No Boundary*.

12. Sengstan, *Verses on the Faith Mind*, trans. R. Clarke (Sharon Springs, N.Y.: Zen Center, 1976).

13. D. Bohm, *Quantum Theory* (Englewood Cliffs, N.J.: Prentice-Hall, 1951), 167.

14. J. Macy, *Despair and Personal Power in the Nuclear Age* (Philadelphia: New Society Publishers, 1983), 25.

15. Ibid., 35.

CHAPTER 8

1. R. Walsh and F. Vaughan, "Towards an Integrative Psychology of Well Being," in *Beyond Health and Normality: Explorations of Exceptional Psychological Wellbeing*, eds. R. Walsh and D. H. Shapiro (New York: Van Nostrand Reinhold, 1983), 388–431.

2. J. Macy, *Despair and Personal Power in the Nuclear Age* (Philadelphia: New Society Publishers, 1983).

3. J. Frank, *Sanity and Survival in the Nuclear Age: Psychological Aspects of War and Peace*, 2nd ed. (New York: Random House, 1982).

4. H. Laughlin, *The Ego and Its Defenses* (New York: Appleton-Century Crofts, 1970).

5. Frank, *Sanity and Survival.*

6. R. Jervis, *Perception and Misperception in Foreign Affairs* (Princeton: Princeton University Press, 1976).

7. Ibid.

8. Frank, *Sanity and Survival.*

9. D. Barash and J. Lipton, *Stop Nuclear War: A Handbook* (New York: Grove, 1982), 227.

10. Confucius, *Confucian Analects, The Great Learning, and the Doctrine of the Mean,* ed. J. Legge (New York: Dover, 1971), 264.

11. R. Lifton, "In a Dark Time," in *The Final Epidemic: Physicians and Scientists on Nuclear War,* eds. R. Adams and S. Cullen (Chicago: Educational Foundation for Nuclear Science, 1981), 7–20.

CHAPTER 9

1. S. Hersch, *The Price of Power* (New York: Summit, 1983).

2. A. H. Maslow, *Toward a Psychology of Being,* 2nd ed. (Princeton: Van Nostrand, 1968), 16.

3. E. Fromm, D. T. Suzuki, and R. DeMartino, *Zen Buddhism and Psychoanalysis* (New York: Harper & Row, 1970), 98.

4. W. Harman, "Old Wine in New Wineskins," in *Challenges of Humanistic Psychology,* ed. J. Bugental (New York: McGraw-Hill, 1962).

5. E. Becker, *The Denial of Death* (New York: Free Press, 1973); and O. Rank, *Beyond Psychology* (New York: Dover, 1958).

6. K. Wilber, *The Atman Project* (Wheaton, Ill.: Quest, 1980); and K. Wilber, *Up From Eden* (New York: Doubleday, 1981).

7. J. Loevinger and E. Knoll, "Personality: Stages, Traits, and the Self." *Annual Review of Psychology* 34 (1983): 195–222.

CHAPTER 10

1. J. Macy, *Despair and Personal Power in the Nuclear Age* (Philadelphia: New Society Publishers, 1983).

2. E. Fromm, "Erich Fromm's Last Interview," *Psychiatric News* 15 (1980): 20.

CHAPTER 11

1. R. Assagioli, *Psychosynthesis: A Manual of Principles and Techniques* (New York: Hohles and Dorman, 1965); A. Ellis, "Rational-emotive Therapy," in *Current Psychotherapies,* ed. R. Corsini (Itasca Ill.: Peacock Press, 1979), 185–229; G. Kelly, *The Psychology of Personal Constructs,* 2 vols. (New York: W. W. Norton, 1955); D. Meichenbaum, *Cognitive-Behavior Modification: An Integrative Approach* (New York: Plenum Press, 1977); and K. Wilber, *The Spectrum of Consciousness* (Wheaton, Ill.: Quest, 1977).

2. O. Markley, "Human Consciousness in Transformation," in *Evolution and Consciousness: Human Systems in Transition,* eds. E. Jantsch and C. Waddington (Reading, Mass.: Addison-Wesley, 1976), 214.

3. E. Jantsch and C. Waddington, eds., *Evolution and Consciousness*; and O. Markley and W. Harman, eds., *Changing Images of Man* (New York: Pergamon, 1982).

4. Markley, "Human Consciousness in Transformation."

5. G. Bateson, *Mind and Nature: A Necessary Unity* (New York: Dutton, 1979), 205.

6. T. Byrom, *The Dhammapada: The Sayings of the Buddha* (New York: Vintage, 1976), 3.

7. A. Globus and G. Globus, "The Man of Knowledge," in *Beyond Health and Normality: Explorations of Exceptional Psychological Wellbeing*, eds. R. Walsh and D. H. Shapiro (New York: Van Nostrand Reinhold, 1983), 294–318.

8. A. Bandura, "Self Efficacy: Toward a Unifying Theory of Behavioral Change," *Psychological Review* 84 (1977): 191–215.

9. J. Levy, "Transpersonal Psychology and Jungian Psychology," *Journal of Humanistic Psychology* 23 (1983): 42–51.

10. R. Walsh and F. Vaughan, "Towards an Integrative Psychology of Well-being," in *Beyond Health and Normality*.

11. J. B. Rotter, "Interpersonal Trust, Trustworthiness, and Gullibility," *American Psychologist* 35 (1980): 1–7.

12. Harvard Nuclear Study Group, *Living With Nuclear Weapons* (New York: Bantam, 1982).

13. J. Frank, *Sanity and Survival in the Nuclear Age: Psychological Aspects of War and Peace*, 2nd ed. (New York: Random House, 1982), 191, 194.

14. H. Willens, *The Trimtab Factor: How Business Executives Can Help Solve the Nuclear Weapons Crisis* (New York: William Morrow, 1983), 34.

15. Frank, *Sanity and Survival*, 282.

16. Satprim, *Sri Aurobindo or the Adventure of Consciousness*, 84.

17. A. Maslow, *Toward a Psychology of Being*.

18. A. Toynbee, *A Study of History*.

CHAPTER 12

1. E. Schumacher, *Small Is Beautiful: Economics as if People Mattered* (New York: Harper & Row, 1973).

2. H. Henderson, *The Politics of the Solar Age* (Garden City, N.Y.: Anchor/Doubleday, 1981).

3. Ibid.

4. D. Elgin, "The Tao of Personal and Social Transformation," in *Beyond Ego: Transpersonal Dimensions in Psychology*, eds. R. Walsh and F. Vaughan (Los Angeles: J. P. Tarcher, 1980), 251–252.

5. I. Yalom, *Existential Psychotherapy* (New York: Basic Books, 1980).

6. H. Marcuse, *An Essay on Liberation* (Boston: Beacon Press, 1969).

7. R. Gregg, cited in Elgin, "The Tao of Personal," 252.

8. Elgin, 252.

9. Longchenpa, *Kindly Bent to Ease Us, Part I: Mind* (Emeryville, Calif.: Dharma, 1975), 143.

10. Elgin, "The Tao of Personal and Social Transformation" and D. Elgin, *Voluntary Simplicity* (New York: William Morrow, 1981).

11. W. Evans-Wentz, *Tibetan Yoga and Secret Doctrines* (London: Oxford University Press, 1935), 80.

12. N. Azrin, B. Naster, and R. Jones, "Reciprocity Counseling: A Rapid Learning-based Procedure for Marital Counseling," *Behavior Research and Therapy* 11 (1973): 365–382.

13. D. Elgin, *The "Communication Rights" Movement: A New Response to National and Global Challenges* (Menlo Park, Calif.: Choosing Our Future, 1983); D. Singer, "A Time to Reexamine the Role of Television in Our Lives," *American Psychologist* 38 (1983): 815–816; and J. Singer and D. Singer, "Psychologists Look at Television: Cognitive, Developmental, Personality, and Social Policy Implications," *American Psychologist* 38 (1983): 826–834.

14. Elgin, *The "Communication Rights" Movement.*

CHAPTER 13

1. C. Osgood, *An Alternative to War or Surrender* (Urbana: University of Illinois Press, 1962).

2. J. Frank, *Sanity and Survival in the Nuclear Age: Psychological Aspects of War and Peace*, 2nd ed. (New York: Random House, 1982), 146.

3. J. Goldstein, *The Experience of Insight* (Boulder, Colo.: Shambhala, 1983); R. Walsh, "The Ten Perfections: Qualities of the Fully Enlightened Individual as Described in Buddhist Psychology," in *Beyond Health and Normality: Explorations of Exceptional Psychological Wellbeing*, eds. R. Walsh and D. H. Shapiro (New York: Van Nostrand Reinhold, 1983), 218–227.

4. Goldstein, *The Experience of Insight.*

5. Goldstein, *The Experience of Insight.*

CHAPTER 14

1. A. H. Maslow, *Toward a Psychology of Being*, 2nd ed. (Princeton: Van Nostrand, 1968); and A. H. Maslow, *The Farther Reaches of Human Nature* (New York: Viking Press, 1971).

2. T. Byrom, *The Dhammapada: The Sayings of the Buddha* (New York: Vintage, 1976), 14.

3. W. Bynner, trans., *The Way of Life According to Lao Tzu* (New York: W. Putnam's Sons, 1944), 65.

4. R. White, "Empathizing with the Rulers of the USSR," *Political Psychology* 4 (1983): 121–137.

CHAPTER 15

1. J. Frank, *Sanity and Survival in the Nuclear Age: Psychological Aspects of War and Peace*, 2nd ed. (New York: Random House, 1982), 224.

2. M. Sherif et al., *Intergroup Conflict and Cooperation: The Robbers' Cave Experiment* (Norman: University of Oklahoma Press, 1961).

3. E. Fromm, *The Art of Loving* (New York: Harper and Row, 1956).

4. R. Hume, *The Thirteen Principal Upanishads* (London: Oxford, 1974).

5. W. Bundy, "On Power: Elements of Power," *Foreign Affairs* 56 (1977): 26.
6. J. Goldstein, *The Experience of Insight* (Boulder, Colo.: Shambhala, 1983), 126.

CHAPTER 16

1. R. Adams and S. Cullen, eds., *The Final Epidemic: Physicians and Scientists on Nuclear War* (Chicago: Educational Foundation for Nuclear Science, 1981); and American Psychiatric Association, *Psychosocial Aspects of Nuclear Developments* (Washington, D.C.: American Psychiatric Association, 1982).
2. American Psychiatric Association, *Psychosocial Aspects*.
3. R. Lifton, *Death in Life: Survivors of Hiroshima* (New York: Random House, 1967).
4. V. Frankl, *Man's Search for Meaning* (New York: Washington Square Press, 1963); and A. Solzhenitsyn, *The Gulag Archipelago, II*, trans. T. Whitney (New York: Harper & Row, 1975).
5. R. May, *The Discovery of Being: Writings in Existential Psychology* (New York: W. W. Norton, 1983); R. Walsh and D. H. Shapiro, eds., *Beyond Health and Normality: Explorations of Exceptional Psychological Wellbeing* (New York: Van Nostrand Reinhold, 1983); R. Walsh and F. Vaughan, eds., *Beyond Ego: Transpersonal Dimensions in Psychology* (Los Angeles: J. P. Tarcher, 1980); and I. Yalom, *Existential Psychotherapy* (New York: Basic Books, 1980).
6. J. Bugental, *Psychotherapy and Process* (New York: Addison-Wesley, 1978); J. Bugental, *The Search for Authenticity*, 2nd ed. (New York: Irvington Publishers, 1981); and J. Goldstein, *The Experience of Insight* (Boulder, Colo.: Shambhala, 1983).
7. F. Perls, *Gestalt Therapy Verbatim* (Lafayette, Calif.: Real People Press, 1969), 16.
8. H. Ansbacher, "Alfred Adler," In *Comprehensive Textbook of Psychiatry*, eds. H. Kaplan, A. Freedman, and B. Sadock, 3rd ed. (Baltimore: Williams and Wilkins, 1980), 729–740; D. Heath, "The Maturing Person," in *Beyond Health and Normality*; A. H. Maslow, *Toward a Psychology of Being*, 2nd ed. (Princeton: Van Nostrand, 1968); A. H. Maslow, *The Farther Reaches of Human Nature* (New York: Viking Press, 1971); R. Walsh, "The Ten Perfections: Qualities of the Fully Enlightened Individual as Described in Buddhist Psychology," in *Beyond Health and Normality*; and A. Waterman, "Individualism and Interdependence," *American Psychologist* 36 (1981): 762–773.
9. J. Frank, *Sanity and Survival in the Nuclear Age: Psychological Aspects of War and Peace*, 2nd ed. (New York: Random House, 1982), 9.
10. Nisargadatta, *I Am That*, 2nd ed., vols. 1 and 2 (Bombay: Chetana, 1976), 140.
11. D. J. Levinson, *The Seasons of a Man's Life* (New York: Knopf, 1978), 242.
12. K. Wilber, *The Spectrum of Consciousness* (Wheaton, Ill.: Quest, 1977).

CHAPTER 17

1. K. Wilber, *Up From Eden* (New York: Doubleday, 1981).
2. A. Aurobindo, *The Future Evolution of Man* (India: All India Press, 1963), 27.
3. B. McWaters, *Conscious Evolution: Personal and Planetary Transformation* (San

Francisco: Institute for the Study of Conscious Evolution, 1981).

4. D. Elgin, "The Tao of Personal and Social Transformation," in *Beyond Ego: Transpersonal Dimensions in Psychology*, eds. R. Walsh and F. Vaughan (Los Angeles: J. P. Tarcher, 1980), 253.

5. C. Rogers, "A Theory of Therapy, Personality, and Interpersonal Relationships as Developed in the Client-centered Framework," in *Psychology: The Study of a Science: Formulations of the Person and the Social Context* (vol. 3) ed. S. Koch (New York: McGraw-Hill, 1959), 184–256.

6. A. H. Maslow, *The Farther Reaches of Human Nature* (New York: Viking Press, 1971), 316–317.

7. I. Yalom, *Existential Psychotherapy* (New York: Basic Books, 1980).

8. S. Taylor, "Adjustment to Threatening Events: A Theory of Cognitive Events," *American Psychologist* 38 (1983): 1161–1173.

9. G. W. Allport, "The Fruits of Eclecticism: Bitter or Sweet," *Acta Psychologica* 23 (1964): 27–44.

10. L. Mumford, *The Transformations of Man* (New York: Harper Brothers, 1956).

11. A. Huxley, *The Perennial Philosophy* (New York: Harper & Row, 1944); H. Smith, *Forgotten Truth* (New York: Harper & Row, 1976); K. Wilber, *Up From Eden* (New York: Doubleday, 1981); and K. Wilber, *A Sociable God: A Brief Introduction to a Transcendental Sociology* (New York: McGraw-Hill, 1983).

12. Walsh, *The Universe Within Us*; K. Wilber, *The Spectrum of Consciousness* (Wheaton, Ill.: Quest, 1977); K. Wilber, *The Atman Project* (Wheaton, Ill.: Quest, 1980); and Wilber, *A Sociable God*.

13. P. Kapleau, *The Three Pillars of Zen* (Boston: Beacon Press, 1965), 143.

14. W. Harman, "An Evolving Society to Fit an Evolving Consciousness," *Integral View* 1 (1979): 14.

15. Wilber, *Up From Eden*; and K. Wilber, ed., *Quantum Questions: The Mystical Writings of the World's Great Physicists* (Boulder, Colo.: New Science Library/Shambhala, 1984).

16. W. James, *William James on Psychical Research*, eds. G. Murphy and R. Ballou (New York: Viking, 1960), 324.

17. Wilber, *Up From Eden*.

18. Elgin, "The Tao of Personal and Social Transformation," 255.

CHAPTER 18

1. D. Elgin, *Voluntary Simplicity* (New York: William Morrow, 1981), 176.

2. R. May, *Man's Search for Himself* (New York: Dell, 1953), 79.

3. T. Byrom, *The Dhammapada: The Sayings of the Buddha* (New York: Vintage, 1976).

4. E. F. Schumacher, *A Guide for the Perplexed* (New York: Harper & Row, 1977).

5. A. Toynbee, *A Study of History* (New York: Oxford University Press, 1934).

6. J. Campbell, *The Hero With a Thousand Faces* (Princeton: Princeton University Press, 1972), 17.

7. R. Walsh and D. H. Shapiro, eds., *Beyond Health and Normality: Explorations of Exceptional Wellbeing* (New York: Van Nostrand Reinhold, 1983).

8. R. S. DeRopp, *The Master Game* (New York: Dell, 1968), 11.

REFERENCES

Adams, R., and Cullen, S., eds. *The Final Epidemic: Physicians and Scientists on Nuclear War*. Chicago: Educational Foundation for Nuclear Science, 1981.

Allport, G. W. "The Fruits of Eclecticism: Bitter or Sweet." *Acta Psychologica*, 23 (1964): 27–44.

American Psychiatric Association. *Psychosocial Aspects of Nuclear Developments*. Washington, D.C.: American Psychiatric Association, 1982.

American Psychological Association. *The Monitor* 14 (1983): 8.

Anonymous. *A Course in Miracles* (text). Tiburon, Calif.: Foundation for Inner Peace, 1975a.

Anonymous. *A Course in Miracles* (workbook). Tiburon, Calif.: Foundation for Inner Peace, 1975b.

Ansbacher, H. "Alfred Adler." In *Comprehensive Textbook of Psychiatry*, edited by H. Kaplan, A. Freedman, and B. Sadock, 3rd ed. Baltimore: Williams and Wilkins, 1980, 729–740.

Assagioli, R. *Psychosynthesis: A Manual of Principles and Techniques*. New York: Hohles and Dorman, 1965.

Aurobindo, A. *The Future Evolution of Man*. India: All India Press, 1963.

Ayres, R. *Banking on the Poor: The World Bank and World Poverty*. Cambridge, Mass.: MIT Press, 1983.

Azrin, N.; Naster, B.; and Jones, R. "Reciprocity Counseling: A Rapid Learning-based Procedure for Marital Counseling." *Behavior Research and Therapy* 11 (1973): 365–382.

Bandura, A. *The Principles of Behavior Modification*. New York: Holt, Rinehart & Winston, 1969.

Bandura, A. "Self Efficacy: Toward a Unifying Theory of Behavioral Change." *Psychological Review* 84 (1977): 191–215.

Barasch, D., and Lipton, J. *Stop Nuclear War: A Handbook*. New York: Grove, 1982.

Barnet, R. "Fantasy, Reality, and the Arms Race: Dilemmas of National Security and Human Survival." *American Journal of Orthopsychiatry* 52 (1983): 582–589.

Bateson, G. *Mind and Nature: A Necessary Unity*. New York: Dutton, 1979.

Becker, E. *The Denial of Death*. New York: Free Press, 1973.

Bereanu, B. "Self Activation of the World Nuclear Weapons System." *Journal of Peace Research* 20 (1983): 49–57.

Bohm, D. *Quantum Theory*. Englewood Cliffs, N.J.: Prentice-Hall, 1951.

Boyle, R. H., and Boyle, R. A. *Acid Rain* (New York: Schocken Books, 1983).

Bracken, P. *The Command and Control of Nuclear Forces*. New Haven: Yale University Press, 1983.

Brandt, W. *North South: A Program for Survival*. Cambridge, Mass.: MIT Press, 1980.

Brown, D. "A Model for the Levels of Concentrative Meditation." *International Journal of Clinical and Experimental Hypnosis* 25 (1977): 236–273.

Brown, D., and Engler, J. "The Stages of Mindfulness Meditation: A Validation Study." *Journal of Transpersonal Psychology* 12 (1980): 143–192.

Brown, L. *Building a Sustainable Society.* New York: W. W. Norton, 1981.

Brown, L. *State of the World.* New York: W. W. Norton, 1984.

Bugental, J. *Psychotherapy and Process.* New York: Addison-Wesley, 1978.

Bugental, J. *The Search for Authenticity,* 2nd ed. New York: Irvington Publishers, 1981.

Bundy, W. "On Power: Elements of Power." *Foreign Affairs* 56 (1977): 1–26.

Bynner, W., trans. *The Way of Life According to Lao Tzu.* New York: W. Putnam's Sons, 1944.

Byrom, T. *The Dhammapada: The Sayings of the Buddha.* New York: Vintage, 1976.

Caldicott, H. *Nuclear Madness: What You Can Do.* Brookline, Mass.: Autumn Press, 1978.

Campbell, J. *The Hero With a Thousand Faces.* Princeton: Princeton University Press, 1972.

Capra, F. *The Turning Point.* New York: Simon & Schuster, 1982.

Carter, L. "WIPP Goes Ahead, Amid Controversy." *Science* 222 (1983): 1102–1104.

Chivian, E., et al., eds. *Last Aid: The Medical Dimension of Nuclear War.* San Francisco: Freeman, 1982.

Confucius. *Confucian Analects, The Great Learning, and the Doctrine of the Mean.* Edited by J. Legge. New York: Dover, 1971.

Conze, E. *Buddhist Meditation.* New York: Harper & Row, 1975.

Council on Environmental Quality. *The Global 2000 Report to the President.* Washington, D.C.: U.S. Government Printing Office, 1979.

Dammann, E. *The Future in Our Hands.* New York: Pergamon, 1979.

David-Neel, A. *Buddhism.* New York: St. Martin's Press, 1939.

Davidson, W. "Psychiatry and Foreign Affairs." *Psychiatric Annals* 13 (1983): 124–133.

Deikman, A. *The Observing Self: Mysticism and Psychiatry.* Boston: Beacon Press, 1982.

DeRopp, R. S. *The Master Game.* New York: Dell, 1968.

Deutch, M. "The Prevention of World War III: A Psychological Perspective." *Political Psychology* 4 (1983): 3–31.

Ehrlich, P.; Harte, J.; and Harwell, M. "Long-Term Biological Consequences of Nuclear War." *Science* 222 (1983): 1293–1300.

Elgin, D. "The Tao of Personal and Social Transformation. In *Beyond Ego: Transpersonal Dimensions in Psychology.* Edited by R. Walsh and F. Vaughan. Los Angeles: J. P. Tarcher, 1980, 248–256.

Elgin, D. *Voluntary Simplicity.* New York: William Morrow, 1981.

Elgin, D. *The "Communication Rights" Movement: A New Response to National and Global Challenges.* Menlo Park, Calif.: Choosing Our Future, 1983.

Ellis, A. "Rational-Emotive Therapy." In *Current Psychotherapies.* Edited by R. Corsini. Itasca, Ill.: Peacock Press, 1979, 185–229.

Eriksen, E. "A Developmental Crisis of Mankind." Talk presented at Physicians for Social Responsibility Meeting, *Prescription for Prevention: Nuclear War—Our Greatest Health Hazard.* Stanford University, October 1983.

Evans-Wentz, W. *Tibetan Yoga and Secret Doctrines.* London: Oxford University Press, 1935.

Ferguson, M. *The Aquarian Conspiracy.* Los Angeles: J. P. Tarcher, 1979.

Frank, J. *Sanity and Survival in the Nuclear Age: Psychological Aspects of War and Peace*, 2nd ed. New York: Random House, 1982.

Frankl, V. *Man's Search for Meaning*. New York: Washington Square Press, 1963.

Freedman, A. "Opiate Dependence." In *Comprehensive Textbook of Psychiatry*, 3rd ed. vol. 2. Edited by H. Kaplan, A. Freedman, and B. Sadock. Baltimore: Williams and Wilkins, 1980, 1591–1614.

Fromm, E. *The Art of Loving*. New York: Harper & Row, 1956.

Fromm, E. "Erich Fromm's Last Interview." *Psychiatric News* 15 (1980): 20.

Fromm, E.; Suzuki, D. T.; and DeMartino, R. *Zen Buddhism and Psychoanalysis*. New York: Harper & Row, 1970.

Fulbright, W. Preface to *Sanity and Survival in the Nuclear Age*, by J. Frank. New York: Random House, 1982, vii–x.

Fuller, B. *Critical Path*. New York: St. Martin's Press, 1981.

Galbraith, J. *The Anatomy of Power*. Boston: Houghton Mifflin, 1983.

Garwin, R., Gottfried, K., and Hafner, D. "Antisatellite Weapons," *Scientific American* 250 (1984): 45–55.

Globus, A., and Globus, G. "The Man of Knowledge." In *Beyond Health and Normality: Explorations of Exceptional Psychological Wellbeing*. Edited by R. Walsh and D. H. Shapiro. New York: Van Nostrand Reinhold, 1983, 294–318.

Goldstein, J. *The Experience of Insight*. Boulder, Colo.: Shambhala, 1983.

Goleman, D. *The Varieties of Meditative Experience*. New York: E.P. Dutton, 1977.

Harman, W. "Old Wine in New Wineskins." In *Challenges of Humanistic Psychology*. Edited by J. Bugental. New York: McGraw-Hill, 1962.

Harman, W. "An Evolving Society to Fit an Evolving Consciousness." *Integral View* 1 (1979): 14.

Harvard Nuclear Study Group. *Living With Nuclear Weapons*. New York: Bantam, 1982.

Health, D. "The Maturing Person." In *Beyond Health and Normality: Explorations of Exceptional Psychological Wellbeing*. Edited by R. Walsh and D. H. Shapiro. New York: Van Nostrand Reinhold, 1983, 152–205.

Henderson, H. *The Politics of the Solar Age*. Garden City, New York: Anchor/Doubleday, 1981.

Hersch, S. *The Price of Power*. New York: Summit, 1983.

Hume, R. *The Thirteen Principal Upanishads*. London: Oxford, 1974.

Huxley, A. *The Perennial Philosophy*. New York: Harper & Row, 1944.

Huxley, A. *Island*. New York: Harper & Row, 1962.

James, W. *William James on Psychical Research*. Edited by G. Murphy and R. Ballou. New York: Viking, 1960.

Jantsch, E., and Waddington, C., eds. *Evolution and Consciousness: Human Systems in Transition*. Reading, Mass.: Addison-Wesley, 1976.

Jervis, R. *Perception and Misperception in Foreign Affairs*. Princeton: Princeton University Press, 1976.

Kahn, H., and Simon, J. *Global 2000 Revised*. Forthcoming.

Kapleau, P. *The Three Pillars of Zen*. Boston: Beacon Press, 1965.

Kelly, G. *The Psychology of Personal Constructs*. 2 vols. New York: W. W. Norton, 1955.

Kerr, R. "The Carbon Cycle and Climate Warming." *Science* 222 (1983): 1107–1108.

Langer, E. "Playing the Middle Against Both Ends: The Usefulness of Adult Cognitive

Activity as a Model for Cognitive Activity in Childhood and Old Age." In *The Development of Reflection*. Edited by S. Yussen. New York: Academic Press, 1982.

Langer, E. *The Psychology of Control*. Beverly Hills, Calif.: Sage, 1983.

Langer, E.; Blank, A.; and Benzion, C. "The Mindfulness of Ostensibly Thoughtful Action: The Role of 'Placebic' Information on Interpersonal Interaction." *Journal of Personality and Social Research* 36 (1978): 635–642.

Laughlin, H. *The Ego and Its Defenses*. New York: Appleton-Century-Crofts, 1970.

Leaning, J., and Keyes, L., eds. *The Counterfeit Ark*. Cambridge, Mass.: Ballinger, 1983.

Levinson, D. J. *The Seasons of a Man's Life*. New York: Knopf, 1978.

Levy, J. "Transpersonal Psychology and Jungian Psychology." *Journal of Humanistic Psychology* 23 (1983): 42–51.

Lewis, K. "The Prompt and Delayed Effects of Nuclear War." *Scientific American* 241 (1978): 35–47.

Lifton, R. *Death in Life: Survivors of Hiroshima*. New York: Random House, 1967.

Lifton, R. "In a Dark Time." In *The Final Epidemic: Physicians and Scientists on Nuclear War*. Edited by R. Adams and S. Cullen. Chicago: Educational Foundation for Nuclear Science, 1981, 7–20.

Lifton, R., and Falk, R. *Indefensible Weapons: The Political and Psychological Case Against Nuclearism*. New York: Basic Books, 1982.

Loevinger, J. and Knoll, E. "Personality: Stages, Traits, and the Self." *American Psychological Review* 34 (1983): 195–222.

Longchenpa. *Kindly Bent to Ease Us, Part I: Mind*. Emeryville, Calif.: Dharma, 1975.

Loup, J. *Can the Third World Survive?* Baltimore: Johns Hopkins University Press, 1983.

Macy, J. *Despair and Personal Power in the Nuclear Age*. Philadelphia: New Society Publishers, 1983.

Marcuse, H. *An Essay on Liberation*. Boston: Beacon Press, 1969.

Markley, O. "Human Consciousness in Transformation." In *Evolution and Consciousness: Human Systems in Transition*. Edited by E. Jantsch and C. Waddington. Reading, Mass.: Addison-Wesley, 1976, 214–229.

Markley, O., and Harman, W., eds. *Changing Images of Man*. New York: Pergamon, 1982.

Maslow, A. H. *Toward a Psychology of Being*, 2nd ed. Princeton: Van Nostrand, 1968.

Maslow, A. H. *The Farther Reaches of Human Nature*. New York: Viking Press, 1971.

May, R. *Man's Search for Himself*. New York: Dell, 1953.

May, R. *The Discovery of Being: Writings in Existential Psychology*. New York: W. W. Norton, 1983.

NcNamara, R. Address to the Board of Governors of the World Bank. Belgrade, 2 October 1979.

McWaters, B. *Conscious Evolution: Personal and Planetary Transformation*. San Francisco: Institute for the Study of Conscious Evolution, 1981.

Meichenbaum, D. *Cognitive-Behavior Modification: An Integrative Approach*. New York: Plenum Press, 1977.

Merton, R. *Social Theory and Social Structure*. Glencoe, Ill.: Free Press, 1957.

Mische, P. *State of the World: A Global Agenda*. Los Angeles: Franciscan Communications, 1981.

110

Mumford, L. *The Transformations of Man*. New York: Harper Brothers, 1956.

National Academy of Sciences. *Resources and Man*. San Francisco: Freeman, 1969.

National Academy of Sciences. *Long-Term Worldwide Effects of Multiple Nuclear-Weapons Detonations*. Washington, D.C.: National Academy of Sciences, 1975.

National Academy of Sciences. *Report of the Carbon Dioxide Assessment Committee*. Washington, D.C.: National Academy Press, 1983.

Nisargadatta. *I Am That*, 2nd ed., vols. 1 & 2. Bombay: Chetana, 1976.

Onosko, T. "Showdown on the High Frontier." *Omni* 6:2 (1983): 73–80.

Osgood, C. *An Alternative to War or Surrender*. Urbana: University of Illinois Press, 1962.

Paine, C. "The Aftermath of Nuclear War." *Science* 220 (1983): 812–814.

Pearl, D.; Bouthilet, L.; and Lazar, J., eds. *Television and Behavior: Ten Years of Scientific Progress and Implications for the Eighties*, vols. 1 & 2. Washington, D.C.: U.S. Government Printing Office, 1982.

Perls, F. *Gestalt Therapy Verbatim*. Lafayette, Calif.: Real People Press, 1969.

Peterson, J., and Hinrichsen, D., eds. *Nuclear War: The Aftermath*. New York: Pergamon, 1982.

Ponnamperuma, "First Word." *Omni* 5:9 (1983): 6.

Population Reference Bureau. *Annual Report*. Washington, D.C.: Population Reference Bureau, 1983.

Presidential Commission on World Hunger. *Preliminary Report of the Presidential Commission on World Hunger*. Washington, D.C.: U.S. Government Printing Office, 1979.

Pressler, L. "First Word." *Omni* 6:2 (1983): 6.

Rank, O. *Beyond Psychology*. New York: Dover, 1958.

Reich, C. *The Greening of America*. New York: Random House, 1970.

Rogers, C. "A Theory of Therapy, Personality, and Interpersonal Relationships as Developed in the Client-Centered Framework." In *Psychology: The Study of a Science, Vol. 3: Formulations of the Person and the Social Context*. Edited by S. Koch. New York: McGraw-Hill, 1959, 184–256.

Rotter, J. B. "Interpersonal Trust, Trustworthiness, and Gullibility." *American Psychologist* 35 (1980): 1–7.

Rubinstein, E. "Television and Behavior: Research Conclusions of the 1982 NIMH Report and Their Policy Implications." *American Psychologist* 38 (1983): 820–825.

Satprem. *Sri Aurobindo, or the Adventure of Consciousness*. New York: Harper & Row, 1968.

Scheer, R. *With Enough Shovels: Reagan, Bush, and Nuclear Wars*. New York: Vintage, 1983.

Schell, J. *The Fate of the Earth*. New York: Knopf, 1982.

Schell, J. "The Abolition: Defining the Great Predicament." *The New Yorker*, January 1984: 36–75.

Schumacher, E. *Small is Beautiful: Economics As If People Mattered*. New York: Harper & Row, 1973.

Schumacher, E. F. *A Guide for the Perplexed*. New York: Harper & Row, 1977.

Seidel, S., and Keyes, D. *Can We Delay a Greenhouse Warming?* Washington, D.C.: U.S. Government Printing Office, 1983.

Sengstan. *Verses on the Faith Mind.* Translated by R. Clarke. Sharon Springs, N.Y.: Zen Center, 1976.

Shapiro, D. H. *Meditation: Self Regulation Strategy and Altered State of Consciousness.* New York: Aldine, 1980.

Sherif, M., et al. *Intergroup Conflict and Cooperation: The Robbers' Cave Experiment.* Norman: University of Oklahoma Press, 1961.

Singer, D. "A Time to Reexamine the Role of Television in our Lives." *American Psychologist* 38 (1983): 815–816.

Singer, J., and Singer, D. "Psychologists Look at Television: Cognitive, Developmental, Personality, and Social Policy Implications." *American Psychologist* 38 (1983): 826–834.

Sivard, R. *World Military and Social Expenditures.* Leesburg, Va.: World Priorities, 1979, 1981, 1983.

Smith, H. *Forgotten Truth.* New York: Harper & Row, 1976.

Solzhenitsyn, A. *The Gulag Archipelago, II.* Translated by T. Whitney. New York: Harper & Row, 1975.

Steinbruner, J. "Launch Under Attack." *Scientific American* 250 (1984): 37–47.

Tart, C. *States of Consciousness.* New York: Dutton, 1975.

Tart, C., ed. *Transpersonal Psychologies.* New York: Harper & Row, 1976.

Taylor, S. "Adjustment to Threatening Events: A Theory of Cognitive Events." *American Psychologist* 38 (1983): 1161–1173.

Time Magazine. January 2, 1984.

Toynbee, A. *A Study of History.* New York: Oxford University Press, 1934.

Turco, R., et al. "Nuclear Winter: Global Consequences of Multiple Nuclear Explosions." *Science,* 222 (1983): 1283–1292.

Union of Concerned Scientists. "Reagan's Star Wars." *New York Review of Books,* April 26, 1984: 47–52.

Van Atta, L. "Arms Control: Human Control." *American Psychologist* 18 (1963): 39.

Walsh, R. "The Consciousness Disciplines and the Behavioral Sciences: Questions of Comparison and Assessment." *American Journal of Psychiatry* 137 (1980): 663–673.

Walsh, R. "The Ten Perfections: Qualities of the Fully Enlightened Individual as Described in Buddhist Psychology." In *Beyond Health and Normality: Explorations of Exceptional Psychological Wellbeing.* Edited by R. Walsh and D. H. Shapiro. New York: Van Nostrand Reinhold, 1983, 218–227.

Walsh, R. "Journey Beyond Belief." *Journal of Humanistic Psychology,* 24 (1984): 30–65.

Walsh, R. *The Universe Within Us.* Forthcoming.

Walsh, R., and Shapiro, D. H., eds. *Beyond Health and Normality: Explorations of Exceptional Psychological Wellbeing.* New York: Van Nostrand Reinhold, 1983.

Walsh, R., and Vaughan, F., eds. *Beyond Ego: Transpersonal Dimensions in Psychology.* Los Angeles: J. P. Tarcher, 1980.

Walsh, R., and Vaughan, F. "Towards an Integrative Psychology of Wellbeing." In *Beyond Health and Normality: Explorations of Exceptional Psychological Wellbeing.* Edited by R. Walsh and D. H. Shapiro. New York: Van Nostrand Reinhold, 1983, 388–431.

Waterman, A. "Individualism and Interdependence." *American Psychologist* 36 (1981): 762–773.

Wedge, B. "Peacemaking." *Psychiatric Annals* 13 (1983): 135–144.

White, R. "Empathizing with the Rulers of the USSR." *Political Psychology* 4 (1983): 121–137.

Wilber, K. *The Spectrum of Consciousness*. Wheaton, Ill.: Quest, 1977.

Wilber, K. *No Boundary*. Los Angeles: Center Press, 1979.

Wilber, K. *The Atman Project*. Wheaton, Ill.: Quest, 1980.

Wilber, K. *Up from Eden*. New York: Doubleday, 1981.

Wilber, K. *A Sociable God: A Brief Introduction to a Transcendental Sociology*. New York: McGraw-Hill, 1983a.

Wilber, K. *Eye to Eye: The Quest for the New Paradigm*. Garden City, N.Y.: Anchor/Doubleday, 1983b.

Wilber, K., ed. *Quantum Questions: The Mystical Writings of the World's Great Physicists*. Boulder, Colo.: New Science Library/Shambhala, 1984.

Willens, H. *The Trimtab Factor: How Business Executives Can Help Solve the Nuclear Weapons Crisis*. New York: William Morrow, 1983.

Woodwell, G., et al. "Global Deforestation: Contribution to Atmospheric Carbon Dioxide." *Science* 222 (1983): 1081–1086.

World Bank. *World Development Report*. Washington, D.C.: U.S. Government Printing Office, 1979.

Yalom, I. *Existential Psychotherapy*. New York: Basic Books, 1980.

APPENDIX

There is strength in numbers, and joining a group of like-minded people committed to similar service-oriented goals can be an inspiring and empowering experience.

The following is a partial list of organizations working toward resolution of current global problems. Many of these organizations have local and international groups. Many other groups exist and can be found in, for example, *The Encyclopedia of Associations*. Many thousands of globally concerned organizations exist worldwide, and it should be possible to find some that match your particular interests and talents. Of course it is wise to take some time and care to investigate a group's intentions and activities before joining.

ORGANIZATIONS CONCERNED WITH MULTIPLE GLOBAL ISSUES

PLANETARY CITIZENS
P.O. Box 2722
San Anselmo, CA 94960
Phone: (415) 485-1545

Promotes the idea of the interdependence of all peoples. Members are registered as "planetary citizens."

GLOBAL TOMORROW COALITION
1525 New Hampshire Ave., N.W.
Washington, DC 20036
Phone: (202) 879-3040

A Coalition of some seventy organizations concerned especially with environmental and natural resource issues.

PEACE CORPS
806 Connecticut Ave., N.W.
Washington, DC 20526
Phone: (202) 254-5010

Volunteers work in countries requiring medical, educational, etc. skills.

ASSOCIATION FOR HUMANISTIC PSYCHOLOGY
325 Ninth St.
San Francisco, CA 94103

Mental health professionals and other interested individuals who share an interest in developing human psychological capacities and wellbeing at individual, social, and global levels.

POPULATION ISSUES

POPULATION ACTION COUNCIL
110 Maryland Ave., N.E., Suite 209
Washington, DC 20002
Phone: (202) 544-3303

Seeks to increase public awareness of global overpopulation problems.

WORLD POPULATION SOCIETY
2213 M Street, N.W., Third Floor
Washington, DC 20037
Phone: (202) 463-6606

Aims to support research and to communicate information about population issues.

ZERO POPULATION GROWTH
1346 Connecticut Ave., N.W.
Washington, DC 20036
Phone: (202) 785-0100

Works for population stabilization in the U.S. and worldwide.

HUNGER AND MALNUTRITION

INTERFAITH HUNGER APPEAL
468 Park Ave. S., Suite 904-A
New York, NY 10016
Phone: (212) 689-8460

An interfaith religious group working to help hungry people develop the skills needed to live self-sufficiently.

OXFAM
115 Broadway
Boston, MA 02116
Phone: (617) 482-1211

Works to help the underprivileged and disaster victims throughout the world to become self-sufficient.

THE HUNGER PROJECT
2015 Steiner St.
San Francisco, CA 94115
Phone: (415) 346-6100

Educational organization aimed at eliminating world hunger by the year 2000.

ECOLOGICAL ISSUES

FRIENDS OF THE EARTH
1045 Sansome St.
San Francisco, CA 94111
Phone: (415) 495-4770

International conservation organization

WORLD POLICY INSTITUTE
777 United Nations Plaza
New York, NY 10017
Phone: (212) 490-0010

Fosters research and provides texts and course outlines for the study and alleviation of war, poverty, social injustice, and ecological destruction.

GREENPEACE
1611 Connecticut Ave. N.W.
Washington, DC 20009
Phone: (202) 462-1177

Concerned with multiple environmental issues. These include protection of the environment and endangered species and the dangers from nuclear testing.

SIERRA CLUB
730 Polk Street
San Francisco, CA 94109
Phone: (415) 776-3036

Concerned with the preservation of the environment.

WORLDWATCH INSTITUTE
1776 Massachusetts Ave. N.W.
Washington, DC 20036
Phone: (202) 452-1999

Analyzes and attempts to anticipate ecological and global problems. Publishes an excellent annual "State of the World" report.

CHOOSING OUR FUTURE
Box 820
Menlo Park, CA 94026
Phone: (415) 853-0600

A group working to make media more responsive to, and information about, global issues.

ISSUES RELATED TO WAR, PEACE, AND NUCLEAR WEAPONS

BEYOND WAR
222 High Street
Palo Alto, CA 94301
Phone: (415) 328-7756

A fast growing group which argues that war is obsolete. Appreciates the importance of psychological factors in understanding and halting the arms race.

COUNCIL FOR A LIVABLE WORLD
100 Maryland Ave. N.E.
Washington, DC 20002
Phone: (202) 543-4100

Works for practical, attainable ways of reducing international tensions and arms. Focuses on the United States Senate.

EDUCATORS FOR SOCIAL RESPONSIBILITY
639 Massachusetts Ave.
Cambridge, MA 02139
Phone: (617) 492-1764

NUCLEAR WEAPONS FREEZE CAMPAIGN
220 I Street, N.E.
Washington, DC 20002
Phone: (202) 544-0880

PHYSICIANS FOR SOCIAL RESPONSIBILITY
639 Massachusetts Ave.
Cambridge, MA 02139
Phone: (617) 924-3468

An organization of physicians and other concerned individuals seeking to educate people about the medical and social costs of the arms race and nuclear war.

INTERNATIONAL PHYSICIANS FOR THE PREVENTION OF NUCLEAR WAR
225 Longwood Ave.
Boston, MA 02115
Phone: (617) 738-9404

This international organization links various national physician groups. It received the 1985 Nobel Peace Prize.

PSYCHOLOGISTS FOR SOCIAL RESPONSIBILITY
1841 Columbia Rd., N.W., Suite 216
Washington, DC 20009
Phone: (202) 745-7084

An organization of psychologists and other concerned individuals who seek to foster understanding and treatment of the psychological factors underlying international tensions, the arms race, and war.

WORLD WITHOUT WAR COUNCIL
1730 Martin Luther King Jr. Way
Berkeley, CA 94709
Phone: (415) 845-1992

Focuses on alternatives to violence capable of advancing the ideas of a free society. Offers research, publications, conferences, and training.

THE PEACE PROJECT
1770 King St.
Santa Cruz, CA 95060
Phone: (408) 425-5061

Educational group working in accord with Christian principles to increase awareness of the nuclear threat.

MOBILIZATION FOR SURVIVAL
853 Broadway, Suite 418
New York, NY 10003
Phone: (212) 533-0008

Coalition of some 150 environmental, women's, community, labor, religious, and peace organizations working together to stop the arms race and meet human needs.

AMERICAN FRIENDS SERVICE COMMITTEE
1501 Cherry St.
Philadelphia, PA 19102
Phone: (215) 241-7000

A Quaker organization whose peace and social work are grounded in "faith in the power of love and nonviolence to bring about change."

119

BAPTIST PEACE FELLOWSHIP
c/o Fellowship of Reconciliation
Box 271
Nyack, NY 10960

CATHOLIC PEACE FELLOWSHIP
339 Lafayette St.
New York, NY 10012
Phone: (212) 673-8990

CLERGY AND LAITY CONCERNED
198 Broadway
New York, NY 10038
Phone: (212) 964-6730

Concerned with human rights and disarmament.

NATIONAL PEACE ACADEMY CAMPAIGN
110 Maryland Ave., N.E., Suite 409
Washington, DC 20002
Phone: (202) 546-9500

Works for legislation to establish a national academy for the study of peaceful ways to avoid and resolve international conflict.

PAX CHRISTI, USA
348 East Tenth Street
Eire, PA 16503
Phone: (814) 453-4955

INTERHELP
Box 331
Northampton, MA 01061
Phone: (413) 586-6311

Aims to empower people to work for planetary survival.

PROFESSIONAL COALITION FOR NUCLEAR ARMS CONTROL
1616 P Street, N.W., Suite 320
Washington, DC 20036
Phone: (202) 332-4823

Political action group of scientists, doctors and lawyers.

Index

Also in New Science Library

Awakening the Heart: East/West Approaches to Psychotherapy and the Healing Relationship, by John Welwood.

Beyond Illness: Discovering the Experience of Health, by Larry Dossey, M.D.

Fisherman's Guide: A Systems Approach to Creativity and Organization, by Robert Campbell.

The Holographic Paradigm and Other Paradoxes. edited by Ken Wilber.

Imagery in Healing: Shamanism and Modern Medicine. by Jeanne Achterberg.

The Inward Arc: Healing and Wholeness in Psychotherapy and Spirituality, by Frances Vaughan.

Jungian Analysis, edited by Murray Stein. Introduction by June Singer.

No Boundary: Eastern and Western Approaches to Personal Growth, by Ken Wilber.

Order Out of Chaos: Man's New Dialogue with Nature, by Ilya Prigogine and Isabelle Stengers. Foreword by Alvin Toffler.

Perceiving Ordinary Magic: Science and Intuitive Wisdom, by Jeremy W. Hayward.

Quantum Questions: Mystical Writings of the World's Great Physicists, edited by Ken Wilber.

A Sociable God: Toward a New Understanding of Religion, by Ken Wilber.

Space, Time and Medicine, by Larry Dossey, M.D.

The Sphinx and the Rainbow: Brain, Mind and Future Vision, by David Loye.

The Tao of Physics: An Exploration of the Parallels between Modern Physics and Eastern Mysticism, second edition, revised and updated, by Fritjof Capra.

Up from Eden: A Transpersonal View of Human Evolution, by Ken Wilber.

The Wonder of Being Human: Our Brain and Our Mind, by Sir John Eccles and Daniel N. Robinson.